A SAFE HAVEN?

A SAFE HAVEN?

A HOMEOWNERSHIP GUIDE TO ASSESSING ENVIRONMENTAL HAZARDS

TODD A. SCHULTZE, CPG

Karlyle Environmental, Inc.
New Jersey

A Safe Haven?
A Homeownership Guide to Assessing
Environmental Hazards
A Karlyle Environmental Book

LIBRARY OF CONGRESS
Library of Congress Card Number:
00-104095

ISBN: 0-615-11338-9

Published by: Karlyle Environmental, Inc.
P.O. Box 902
Dover, NJ 07801

Printed in the United States of America

1 3 5 7 9 10 8 6 4 2

To Theresa and Lauren, the lights in so many lives.
You are treasured.

CONTENTS

LIST OF FIGURES AND TABLES

PREFACE AND ACKNOWLEDGEMENTS

This book has been written for homeowners, prospective homeowners, and for anyone else that may have concerns about protecting their health and the health of their families. Issues such as poor indoor air quality, lead-based paint, water supply contamination, and hazardous wastes, mean that our homes and communities may not be as safe as we would like to think. The intent of this book is to provide you with information that is necessary to be able to recognize environmental hazards in and around your home, and to understand options that are available to reduce or eliminate the associated risks. Prospective homebuyers can apply the information as a guide to investigate environmental issues, and then be able to assess the relative safety of homes and communities before purchase.

After almost twenty years of environmental geology education and consulting experience, I have found that the public's response to environmental issues varies considerably. While some homeowners can obsess about or be completely perplexed by possible hazards, others may never give them a second thought based on the false belief that environmental hazards are something confined solely to industrial and urban areas. These reaction extremes are usually due to misunderstandings of or an absence of accurate information.

Our concerns about environmental risks must be based in reality – fact and science. We need to be informed to allow a realistic assessment of a hazard and a well-founded decision on how to deal with the risk. The degree and method of a hazard investigation will depend on the type of environmental concern, the associated risk, and the level of resources you want to devote to the investigation. Other factors that may influence the investigation process can include the accessibility to historical information, availability of time, physical site characteristics, and the technology that is accessible to conduct the assessments.

It is important to recognize that in a home environment, the assessment of risk associated with environmental hazards becomes a continual process. Because our environment and our health are in a constant state of change, so too must our assessment of possible exposures be periodically re-evaluated.

Our potential for exposure to and adverse impacts from environmental hazards varies based on our age, lifestyles, choice of home, socioeconomic status, area of the country, and even dumb luck. Because each instance of possible exposure will represent a unique set of circumstances, this book is not designed to be a replacement for specific investigations and testing; rather it is meant to be a starting point.

The chapters of the book that focus on particular hazards are loosely divided into three general sections. These are: a discussion of the magnitude of the problem and the health consequences, how to assess the risk by evaluating the particular conditions and possible exposure routes, and lastly how to mitigate hazards. There is overlap between the issues presented in some of the chapters because you will find that exposure routes, like breathing indoor air and drinking water, can be impacted by numerous contaminant sources. Some of these sources deserve expanded and specific discussions, and therefore, separate chapters were written.

This book has been a labor of love. I am very grateful to M. L. Schultze, whose professional editing skills and economy of words reminded me of the value of getting to the point. I trust that you will find the information helpful in giving perspective on the range of possible concerns and how and when it becomes necessary to take action. I also hope that it will raise an awareness of issues not typically considered in a home environment.

Todd A. Schultze, CPG

A SAFE HAVEN?

INTRODUCTION

Since the early 1980s, environmental concerns have become increasingly prevalent and an inescapable component to the ownership of residential property. Environmental issues represent perhaps the single most important area of uncertainty and risk in the area of residential real estate. Changing attitudes toward personal health, and the health of the environment, have led to a greater awareness of these problems.

More than just dollars, environmental problems can effect your health, the health of your family and guests, and even pets. From radon contamination to leaking oil tanks, from drinking water to lead, many environmental issues are potential catastrophes awaiting the uninformed. In these times, it is prudent and necessary to investigate residential property for a wide range of environmental problems, to avoid the heartache and considerable expense when problems arise. The cost of correcting a problem, after you buy a home, can be significant, ranging from a few hundred dollars to vent radon to hundreds of thousands of dollars to remediate contaminated soil and groundwater.

Purchasing a home is typically the largest single expenditure a family can expect to make in their lifetime. It can be an exhilarating and nerve-wracking experience with potential pitfalls that can trap the unwary, whether you are a first-time homebuyer or the savvy veteran of real estate purchasing. In almost no other transaction does the phrase *caveat emptor* - 'let the buyer beware' - carry so much weight.

In many states, existing homeowners, as well as prospective real estate purchasers and sellers, must investigate a myriad of potential concerns to ensure the absence of environmental hazards and the associated health risks. Awareness of the potential problems inherent in the ownership of a home is the important first step to minimizing risks. Whether buying or living in your first home or your fifth, a vacation home or rental property, a mansion or a cottage, you should be informed of the threats posed by environmental issues.

This book compiles in one place most every environmental issue a homeowner needs to be aware of and serves as a guide to help families lead safer lives. While it cannot detail or discuss every example of risky conditions, it provides an overview to the most common and most important issues you should be aware of and investigate.

In straightforward language you are presented with each area of environmental concern and provided a summary of the problems that can be encountered, the health and/or monetary consequences of these problems, and clear direction on what to look for and what to avoid. A survey questionnaire allows you to begin the assessment process to evaluate your present home or to ask the right questions before you decide to buy a home and sign a contract that may not protect you from these problems.

This book is not intended as a substitute for the professional services of an attorney, environmental consultant or real estate agent. It should be considered as a reference source of information - a primer - to help you undertake the proper investigations prior to purchasing or selling a home, or to evaluate the safety of your existing home.

Richard J. Kapner, Esq.

A FINE MESS

"One's home is the safest refuge to everyone."
Pandects (Roman Civil Law)

"Here are a few of the unpleasant'st words that ever blotted paper."
William Shakespeare

INTRODUCTION

Is it enough to consider only the quality of schools, crime rates, taxes and the size of a backyard when looking for a new home? Should you have concerns about undetected environmental hazards in homes and communities, despite the fact that homeowners have lived under those conditions for decades? Is it now necessary to assess homes with respect to potential health risks, thereby establishing a whole new set of criteria for whether a home is an acceptable and safe place to live?

You can no longer assume that harmful exposures to hazardous materials and toxic environments will occur only in industrial areas, urban areas, or at a place of employment. Increasingly, we must look within our homes, neighborhoods and communities for some of the most likely sources of exposures to environmental contaminants. We spend most of our lives sleeping, eating, drinking and simply breathing in our homes. Because of this concentration of time, our homes and their surroundings, under the right conditions, can represent significant sources of direct and adverse impacts to our health.

When you evaluate the risk associated with exposures to hazardous environments, the duration of exposure, route of exposure, and type and concentration of the contaminants are primary factors that determine the risks to our health. It should also be considered that our lifestyles and environments are in a constant state of change, both in and outside the home. Therefore, the level of risk can constantly change.

Accordingly, an assessment of risk must take into account not only the known conditions, but also the potential for changes in our surroundings that may alter our exposure levels. If we find, for example, that lead-based paint exists in a home, the risk associated with exposure to the paint may fluctuate depending on the use of a home or the age of its occupants. In the instance of contaminants in drinking water, the associated risk can increase over time due to an accumulation of toxic materials in the body, changes in health, or changes in the migration and concentration of contaminants.

CAUSE FOR CONCERN

Environmental hazards: tainted drinking water, poor indoor and outdoor air quality, dangerous housing materials, contaminated groundwater and surface water, bacteriological and radioactive hazards, hazardous waste discharges, underground storage tank leaks, accidental toxic material releases, the list goes on and on. The impacts to our health: headaches, nausea, severe allergic reactions, birth defects, impaired mental and physiological development, heightened chemical sensitivities, cancers, respiratory disorders, death, the list goes on and on.

Where are the risks?   Unfortunately, the question may be more easily answered by asking where *aren't* the risks?   Exposures to environmental hazards can occur at places of work, at play, and in our homes. Given that we spend the majority of our lives in and around our homes, it is ironic that what should be a safe haven can often represent the area of greatest risk to our health.

The issue of environmental hazards in the home is especially relevant for children, who, during their developmental stages and because of higher respiratory rates, are often the most susceptible to contaminants in the surrounding environment.   Our vulnerability to pollutants is most often a dose-related condition - the higher the relative exposure concentration, the greater the harm.   For that reason, smaller children can often suffer greater damage by a lower exposure dose of contaminants.

A house in and of itself can be hazardous. Building materials such as lead-based paint, asbestos insulation, and even certain types of wood products can cause health problems. Naturally occurring radon can infiltrate a home and adversely impact air and water quality.   Contaminated soil and other fill materials on which a home is built, or the migration of contaminants from off-site sources through the air, soil, surface water, or groundwater may also represent health problems for homeowners and their families.   Figure 1.1 illustrates the "cycle" of contaminants and the avenues for human exposure.

Ultimately, we find that environmental hazards originate from both natural and manmade sources. Because of the multiple sources of hazards and the fact that we are often dealing with something that is not fully understood and usually something that we cannot even see, misunderstandings and fears of the unknown are common when addressing environmental hazards.   For many potential contaminant situations, this lack of information or even misinformation often cause panicked actions or a failure to act – both of which can be dangerous.

Concerns about the environmental safety of a home often extend well beyond the residents of a home, and can include neighbors, realtors, banks and other lenders. An increasing awareness of environmental hazards has made many

A SAFE HAVEN?

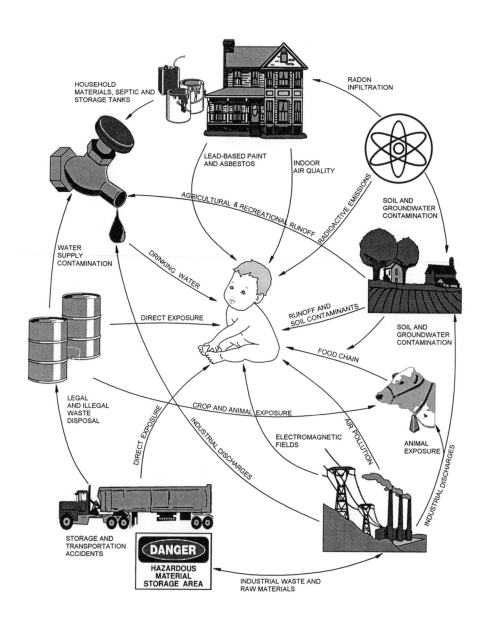

FIGURE 1.1 - CONTAMINANT "CYCLE" AND HUMAN EXPOSURE ROUTES

lenders skittish over the past fifteen years. These apprehensions often result in banks requiring property inspections and assessments to minimize their potential for assuming environmental liability if they are forced to foreclose.

A SAD STATE OF AFFAIRS

Hundreds of new chemical compounds, in the form of raw materials and vast quantities of waste, are released into the air, land, and water each year. Thousands of major and minor petroleum spills and leaks occur across the United States every year. Decades of rapid military development and careless storage and disposal have left thousands of contaminated sites across millions of acres of land. Municipal water supplies are routinely shut down because they become unfit for drinking. In many cases, to make water potable again, extensive treatment procedures become necessary to remove contaminants.

Discharges of chemical, radioactive and biological wastes produce acute and chronic impacts to the environment and to our health. In some circumstances, we find ourselves becoming sick immediately in response to a discharge and exposure. This reaction is due to the acute toxicity of the contaminant. Alternatively, we may find that illnesses can develop over time, only to be ultimately traced back to an exposure that was previously unknown. Not only does our society continuously create new environmental hazards, but the contaminants that were discharged in the past are analogous to time bombs that all too often are not identified until the bombs have gone off.

Our problems exist above, on and beneath the earth. Sadly, it has become commonplace to rate the quality of our air and issue respiratory advisories on the evening news. It is now routine for many metropolitan areas to tabulate yearly totals for the number of "unhealthy" air days. Health professionals regularly advise us to keep children, older people and those with respiratory ailments indoors during "bad air" and ozone alert days.

Former and active industrial zones in every state are virtually toxic wastelands. Due to the contamination of soil and groundwater, the value of these properties is often less than zero. In every state, hundreds of miles of rivers and hundreds of lakes are classified as unfit for drinking, swimming, and fishing.   Groundwater, used for drinking water by about half the population of the United States, is highly vulnerable to contamination from an almost infinite number of sources.   Over the years we have been forced to accept that pure drinking water is no longer the norm, and that we must tolerate maximum contaminant levels (MCLs) for dozens of chemicals.

HAZARDS CLOSE TO HOME

Historically, environmental pollution was a problem that for the most part was localized in urban zones and areas of industrial manufacturing and waste disposal sites.   However, as human population and industry exploded with increasing demands for more this and better that, industry, raw materials and wastes moved closer to home and vice versa.   Industrial and commercial use of hazardous materials followed the population shift to the suburbs. Due to high property values, a lack of space, and a desire to live near work and other conveniences, we have found an ever expanding and intermingling of industrial, commercial, disposal, and residential zones. Dramatic population growth over the past 100 years created a vicious cycle of more need, more production, more waste, and as a final result - the potential for more harmful exposures to environmental contaminants in and around the home.

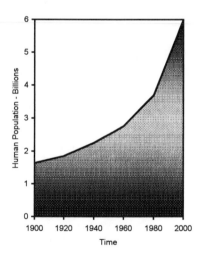

It must also be realized that the vast quantities and types of chemicals and wastes that we produce have the ability to migrate. This migration can occur through the air, soil, surface water, or groundwater. As a consequence, we must consider not just the obvious potential hazards that are near our homes, but also those hazards that can migrate from greater distances.   We find therefore, that a water supply can become contaminated from a pollutant source that is miles away, and air quality can be impacted from sources that are several states away.

Under these circumstances, it has become increasingly necessary to identify and assess the possible hazards in and around homes, evaluate the health risk and if practical, eliminate it. At the same time, however, we must remember to keep our perspective rooted in reality and not based on misplaced fear caused by misunderstandings of the real risk. Can you eliminate all exposures and, therefore, all potential risks to your health? Probably not. At least not in the world of modern chemicals, conveniences, and throwaway lifestyles to which we have become accustomed. However, it is possible to gather information that will help us take corrective measures where appropriate. Information on risks also allows comparisons and evaluations of the relative safety of one home or community versus another, thereby, providing a means to minimize our exposures.

RECOGNIZING AND REGULATING THE PROBLEM

Until about twenty-five years ago, the general public's concerns about environmental pollution were primarily limited to smog, litter, and obvious waste dumped into oceans, lakes, and streams. Concerns, if they existed at all, were most often associated with pollution that was readily apparent. Issues of chemical, biological and radioactive contamination (which typically were present at levels that could be detected only in the laboratory) were unfamiliar to most people.

However, as extreme cases of environmental contamination made the news – chemical waste sites blowing sky high, unexplained clusters of illnesses, Love Canal in New York, contamination of drinking water supplies – public support and demand for action increased dramatically. People recognized that the government's responsibility for safeguarding public health had to extend beyond fire and police protection. Regulations became necessary to educate and protect the public from newly recognized hazards both in and outside the home.

The United States Environmental Protection Agency (USEPA), formed in 1970, passed new laws and strengthened existing ones to regulate environmental health issues and the handling and disposal of wastes. Many states followed with their own regulations. State agencies, previously devoted to natural resource development, geological surveys, and the like, evolved into departments to preserve and clean up the environment and to regulate toxic materials. New federal and state regulations were rapidly implemented to govern disposal methods, industrial operations and the cleanup of years of contamination problems that were rapidly, and in some cases literally, coming to the surface.

One adverse and unintended consequence of the new environmental awareness and regulations, was that, as unscrupulous waste generators and handlers saw what was coming down the regulatory pike, indiscriminate and illegal "midnight dumping" skyrocketed. Industry and haulers resorted to these practices to avoid the inevitable increases in disposal costs that went with compliance. The result was haphazard disposal of wastes with no true records of what went where.

To a small degree, the carelessness of the past can be justified by saying that we just did not know. The short and long-term effects of toxic chemicals on humans and the environment had never been extensively studied. It was also incorrectly assumed that the capacity of the earth, to absorb and ultimately cleanse the wastes that we discharged and buried, was infinite. It was not widely understood that hazardous materials and wastes endure, and, when released into the environment, they were going where they would ultimately cause long lasting harm and taint the air we breathe, the food we eat, and the water we drink. Only a small percentage of waste material was disposed of in what is now considered a safe manner.

Errors occurred (sometimes conveniently) before the hazards were fully understood. Nevertheless, there is no excuse now, and unfortunately, we continue to make many of the same mistakes. The careless practices of the past continue to be repeated by industry and disposal facilities as well as by John Q. Public around the home. In residential communities, it is common to encounter excessive pesticide and herbicide use, dumping in storm drains, leaking underground tanks, air quality problems, and tainted drinking water. Additionally, we have come to the slow realization that health threats originate not only from unusual industrial chemicals, but from natural sources in the earth and from common construction and finishing materials that have been used for years to build and to furnish our homes.

ASSESSING THE CONCERNS

"So long as the mother, Ignorance, lives, it is not
safe for Science, the offspring,
to develop the hidden causes of things."

Johannes Kepler

OPENING A CAN OF WORMS

The investigation of a home and property, for one or a combination of potential environmental hazards, can vary in complexity. The degree and method of an investigation depends upon the type of environmental concern, the associated risk, and the level of resources you want to devote to the investigation. Other factors include the accessibility to historical information, the availability of time, the physical site characteristics, and the accessible technology to conduct the assessments.

Regardless of the type of hazard, the primary question that must be addressed is: What level of risk is acceptable? Property investigations and risk assessments may not be a consideration at all if you don't mind uncertainty. The absence of a vulnerable lifestyle, a lack of concern, or other factors may support a high level of risk-tolerance. Alternatively, people with low or no tolerance for risk would generally want a considerable degree of investigation to address their concerns. This low tolerance can stem from health susceptibilities, anxiety over the known as well as the unknown, and vulnerable lifestyles.

WHO IS RESPONSIBLE?

In the case of real estate transfers, the issue of responsibility for site and home investigations is often a sticking point. Sellers may take the position that it is up to the buyers to satisfy themselves that there are no environmental concerns associated with a property. At the same time, however, a seller may not want "outsiders" randomly conducting investigations in a home or across a piece of developed or undeveloped property that could open a can of worms. The impartiality of professionals that are brought into the project is an issue that also needs to be considered. Are a potential buyer and his paid investigators making mountains out of molehills solely for price negotiation purposes? Alternatively, are the findings produced by a seller's investigators trustworthy or is something being concealed?

With respect to homeowners who have concerns about their property being contaminated from historical or from off-site sources, the problem of responsibility for the investigations must be weighed against a need to be informed. Your paying for a potentially expensive and complicated investigation of a property may seem unjust, especially when the suspected source of the contamination comes from some other party. Unfortunately, when investigating a property, proving responsibility for contamination, and in subsequent attempts to force reparation, the burden often falls (at least initially) upon the innocent impacted parties.

Under certain circumstances, a homeowner may be notified that their property or water source has become contaminated. A homeowner then needs to question whether they are more comfortable gathering their own data or whether to trust information from someone responsible for the contamination or if they can put faith in regulatory agencies that may conduct the investigations.

There are also sad circumstances where, despite prior and supposedly careful investigations, major sources of contaminants have not been identified. In the case of a former manufacturing building outside New York City (that was being renovated into residential units), professional consultants had inspected the property before purchase by the future residents. Additionally, based on the data generated in the investigations, the state environmental agency had given clearance for the sale. Nevertheless, mercury contamination was later identified throughout portions of the building and several residents were found to be suffering from mercury poisoning. Unfortunately, there is no guarantee when dealing with environmental contaminants

RISK EVOLUTION

Regardless of the level of risk you are willing to accept, it is important to recognize that the assessment of risk is a continual and evolutionary process. Before any investigation, decisions are made as to how intensive the inquiries and explorations will be – again this is based in large part on tolerance for risk. As you are gathering information, the risk-assessment process must continue and evolve. Concerns and tolerance levels may then be modified. You may decide no further investigation or corrective action is warranted. Alternatively, you may want to expand the scope. Insofar as the environment, our families, our lifestyles, and our own health are in a constant state of change, so too must our assessment of the hazards be re-evaluated periodically and adapted to new conditions if necessary.

Aside from our own tolerance levels for risk, other factors influence the degree to which, if any, an investigation may be conducted. Certainly, due to the varying degrees of contaminant toxicities, some investigations will be more critical and have deeper ramifications than others. Concerns over chlorinated hydrocarbon contamination of our drinking water, in almost every case, would be more important than a potential asbestos problem.

The potential for exposure also determines whether detailed investigations are necessary or whether simple avoidance is the solution. Site-specific conditions such as geology and home construction will likewise be major factors in determining the need for, as well as the approach to, investigations of environmental hazards. Lastly, our financial resources will have a significant influence over the degree to which investigations and corrective measures can be taken.

NO SILVER BULLET

Recognize that, depending upon the type of environmental concern, there is no investigation method that can answer all questions for all potential circumstances. At the same time, it is not feasible to expect a "silver bullet" could provide constant safeguards against all environmental hazards. This is due to changing environmental conditions as well as the practicalities of everyday life.

For example, it is unreasonable to deliver samples of your tap water to an analytical laboratory on a daily basis for complete testing. On the other hand, it is just as irrational simply to assume that there is no potential for contaminant exposure and to expect complete isolation from hazardous substances. Some circumstances dictate that a certain amount of risk is inevitable. We need to consider what is practical and reasonable.

WHOM CAN YOU CALL?

Not to worry - A vast network of professionals are available to inspect, sample, test, dig, drill, monitor, interview, analyze, research, compute and report to help you evaluate the environmental risks of a home and property. These professionals encompass contractors, home inspectors, geologists, engineers, laboratories and consultants, who will all (for a fee) assist you to determine, reduce, and possibly eliminate the risks.

In addition, local, state, and federal authorities represent vast resources of information in print, on the Internet, and verbally to help homeowners in assessing possible concerns. Aside from the professionals and regulators, your own commonsense can go a long way to providing answers. The best part of that is it is free. Do not underestimate your own abilities to do a little research and know what to look for. In fact, it is vital for you to maintain a working understanding of environmental issues to allow informed and intelligent decisions about the need for and type of investigation and corrective action or maintenance. The common concerns associated with a home environment are summarized in the following sections. The Appendix questionnaire is a preliminary home survey for use after completing the book.

RADON

The geology of an area, the type of home construction, and the amount of ventilation, all affect the degree to which radon may concentrate within a home. Over the years, radon accumulation has become a more prevalent problem because of increasingly energy-efficient and "tight" homes. Radon levels will vary as a result of seasonal ventilation, changes in atmospheric pressure, temperature and precipitation. Inherent variations in geology and building construction will cause wide differences in radon levels to develop within a small geographic area. Radon levels or the lack thereof in a neighbor's home should not be taken as an indication of the potential levels in your own home.

If you are in the market for a house, conduct at least one radon test. Some localities require the test before issuing a certificate of occupancy. The Environmental Protection Agency says all residences with living areas below the third-floor level should be tested for radon. In an effort to represent worst case conditions, testing should be conducted during colder months when the home is subject to the least amount of ventilation. Testing in below ground locations, such as basements, will typically identify the highest concentrations in a home.

Professional testing companies can be retained to place the radon sensors and interpret the results. Alternatively, testing can be done with relatively inexpensive kits that you can purchase at home supply stores or through mail order. Short-term kits and long-term kits range in test periods from a matter of days to as much as three months. Long-term kits typically average out abnormal highs and lows. As much care as possible should be taken to ensure that the results are representative of actual day to day living conditions.

In most cases, the correction of a radon problem is simple and involves reducing concentrations by venting or by dilution with outside air. New home construction should incorporate radon resistant building methods.

LEAD

Investigations to determine the presence of lead in your home are important. They are especially vital if children may be exposed. Potential exposures are from lead-based paint and the dust that is created as it ages, as well as from lead in water supplies. However, if a home was built after 1988, the potential for lead to be present in paint or in water pipes is significantly reduced.

Screening kits for lead-based paint detection are available in most hardware stores. The costs are generally minor and the testing kits are relatively easy to use. Somewhat more sophisticated mail-order tests are also available. Professional investigators can use test kits or more advanced x-ray fluorescence machines. X-ray fluorescence can produce a relatively quick and complete survey of an entire home. Regardless of the method used, the procedure should take into account the potential for multiple layers of paint that are typically found in older homes.

Testing for lead in drinking water can be somewhat more involved than testing lead-based paint. The concentrations of lead in the water can be determined by submitting a sample of your water to a health department or a qualified analytical laboratory, or by having the laboratory or a consultant do the sampling. The most common cause for lead in drinking water is due to household pipes and pipe connections. Water that sits for at least several hours in pipes, which include a lead component, will represent the worst case levels of lead. For that reason, flushing the pipes before you drink the water is an effective way to reduce lead levels.

AIR QUALITY

Poor interior air quality is a primary source of adverse health impacts for many people. Problems with air quality in and around your home can originate from building materials, furnishings, excessive moisture, discharges of waste materials, improper venting of combustion devices, migration of underground contaminant plumes, and local and regional air pollution. Concerns over air quality usually arise because of unusual odors, respiratory problems, and/or from knowing about a contaminant source with a potential air quality component.

Because the sources of problems vary so widely, so do the investigation methods of air quality in your home. Fortunately, your nose knows and often detects problems at odor thresholds that are much lower than the levels at which your health can be damaged. Home reconnaissance should be thorough, looking and smelling for potential problem areas. Monitors such as carbon monoxide detectors are a good idea for any home where combustion occurs (which is virtually every home in the United States). A licensed heating contractor can be retained to inspect for the proper operation of furnaces and venting systems.

Sampling tubes and professional monitoring instruments are available to take instantaneous measurements of contaminant concentrations throughout a home. Samples of air can also be collected for laboratory analyses to identify specific types of volatile compounds or other contaminants. A professional can ensure proper investigation procedures such as appropriate locations, sampling rates and sampling volumes.

Individuals with heightened sensitivities to chemicals such as formaldehyde should inspect a home carefully to ensure that formaldehyde-free materials are used in construction and furnishings. Natural-fiber carpet or tile and wood floors can also eliminate potential sources of volatile vapors that can be present in some synthetic carpets.

Although significant improvements in outdoor air quality have been measured over the past twenty-five years, about one-half of the U.S. population still lives in areas where acceptable air quality standards are regularly exceeded. Assessments of problems with exterior air quality should focus on the degree and type of industrialization and commercialization, together with the topographic features of an area. All other things being equal, due to the geographic isolation by surrounding mountains and hill, homes in heavily developed valleys tend to be exposed to higher concentrations of air pollutants. Areas of the country with relatively stagnant weather patterns also typically have higher air pollution levels. On a local level, you can investigate the area surrounding your home to determine whether the property is downwind (given prevailing patterns) from potential sources.

HAZARDOUS MATERIALS

The presence of hazardous materials throughout our environment often warrants significantly expanded levels of property investigation. Homeowners must consider the potential for exposure to toxic materials by migration of buried wastes, material storage accidents, and intentional discharges. Additionally, as communities become increasingly developed and turn over on themselves, we find homes have been built on or often very near previously deposited hazardous materials and wastes.

When evaluating a home you own or may buy, and the associated potential for exposure to hazardous materials and waste, you must consider the locations of manufacture, storage, usage, disposal, and treatment, as well as uncontrolled waste sites. Basic research at local chambers of commerce and a simple area reconnaissance can provide a wealth of information on the types and volume of industry and waste production in an area. The investigation is aided by data from Community Right-to-Know information. You can then make educated and informed decisions about what you want or do not want in (or beneath) your backyard.

Assessing the threat that a type of industry may present to a community must also consider the avenues of exposure. The medium (air, soil or water) to which releases occur will be a primary factor in determining the potential for your exposure. The resulting assessment may decide for example, that an industry that releases wastes to the air represents less of a concern than an industry whose discharges could enter surface water or groundwater supplies.

DRINKING WATER

All water is at risk of contamination. Investigating household water quality can be a series of complicated steps, although, in all cases it begins with a simple taste, odor and visual inspection. A review of local newspapers can disclose violation notices of public water suppliers. You can also get copies of required testing results by direct requests to the water utility. Local health departments, state agencies and the EPA can provide additional quality information on public and private water supplies for any community.

Evaluation of the water quality of a region, and the potential for contamination, must take into account the wide spectrum of possible pollutant sources. Water contaminants originate from everywhere - from simple residential and agricultural runoff to discharges from heavy industry. The heightened vulnerability of water supplies is due to the ability of small concentrations of contaminants to migrate significant distances and to pollute vast quantities of water. Further assessments of your home water quality must consider the advantages and disadvantages associated with both public and private water service and whether the source is a surface supply or a groundwater supply.

Property purchases that include a private well should be, and in many cases must be, investigated with a thorough round of laboratory analyses. In this day and age, simple potability criteria such as hardness and pH are not enough. The potential for chemical and other contamination must also be a real consideration. An independent certified laboratory or consultant are best qualified to perform water sampling. When problems are indicated, the results must be evaluated carefully, and if necessary, verified through repeat testing before you take corrective actions.

Treatment options for drinking water problems should all be considered temporary measures. The cost and required maintenance activities of water treatment technologies can be high, and yet, no system is foolproof. The only permanent solution to water quality problems is to eliminate the source(s) of contamination and/or to convert to a substitute water supply.

STORAGE TANKS

Discharges from petroleum storage tanks represent one of the most common causes of soil and groundwater contamination, and therefore, possible human exposures. Interior odor and air quality problems can also result from storage tank leaks. Due to the high potential for discharges, many lenders require the investigation of a storage tank before they will give you a mortgage or provide refinancing. Therefore, investigations for unknown tanks and the assessment of the condition of active tanks are important. Aboveground tanks are easily inspected for signs of leaks or spills. A property should also be carefully examined for indications of former underground tanks.

In many cases, whether or not the integrity of an underground tank is assessed should depend on decisions about the continued need for the tank. If you plan to replace the tank or convert to another heating source, you still should inspect the tank after closure. If you plan to keep using a tank, checking for impacts to the environment is best evaluated by soil or possibly groundwater sampling. The findings determine, ultimately, if you will remove the tank.

Methods for finding out if your tank is leaking vary and the data collected from the procedures can represent a number of possible conditions. The site-specific circumstances dictate which method is best. An observational approach that considers the age and contents of the tank, heating system operation, and any known soil or groundwater conditions can provide an educated guess about the likely integrity findings.

In the case of real estate transfers, the issue of financial responsibility for tank investigations and removal should become a point of negotiation on the purchase price. Depending on the investigation results, either or both parties may decide to call off the sale or consider further financial adjustments.

ASBESTOS

Although significant health hazards have been demonstrated in association with occupational exposures to asbestos, most data indicate that typical residential levels are of limited concern. Regardless of the type of asbestos, it can only be a hazard if it is physically disturbed, thereby allowing fibers to become airborne and possibly inhaled. Close proximity to undisturbed material does not represent a health risk.

If materials in the home are suspected of containing asbestos, samples can be collected and analyzed to determine the asbestos type and amount. Professionals should perform the sampling of materials inasmuch as improper technique can result in the unintended release of airborne fibers and/or non-representative samples. Additionally, if the presence of asbestos containing materials has been confirmed, sampling of air can be conducted to address the question of whether fibers are indeed becoming airborne under normal living conditions.

The risk associated with asbestos materials in the home depends entirely on the physical condition of the material and the potential for disruption and degradation. Home surveys should assess suspect and confirmed asbestos material with respect to integrity, accessibility, and the potential for future disruption or damage. If an abatement of asbestos materials has been conducted, follow-up air sampling is necessary. An improperly conducted abatement can release many times more fibers than would have existed without the removal.

A RISKY BUSINESS

"There are in fact two things, science and opinion; the former begets knowledge, the latter ignorance."

Hippocrates

EXPOSURE ASSESSMENTS AND HEALTH EFFECTS

Though hazardous environments may exist in our homes and communities, there could be no adverse health impact if we weren't exposed to the contaminants. In almost all cases, the risk and effect from an environmental hazard is dose-related. As the concentration of a contaminant or the duration of exposure increases, so too does the risk.

If we choose therefore, to minimize the potential for health risks by avoiding hazards, it is important to understand the routes of potential exposure. Human exposure to environmental contaminants generally occurs in one of four ways:

Inhalation – breathing contaminated dusts, vapors, fibers, gases or fumes into your lungs. Examples include inhaling asbestos fibers, radon gas, or organic chemical vapors and mists.   Depending on an individual's susceptibility and the type of contaminant, the impacts of inhalation may be immediate such as irritation and swelling of the airway passages and labored breathing.   Alternatively, the health effects may not occur for some time, eventually resulting in disorders like emphysema and lung cancer.

Ingestion – pollutants can be consumed in the form of dust that is swallowed, such as when children put their dirty fingers or items into their mouths, or when airborne dust particles land in the mouth.   Eating tainted food and drinking contaminated water also results in ingesting pollutants.   Because either odor or taste would usually detect high concentrations of contaminants, this type of exposure usually occurs at low levels over long periods.   The health effects can include liver and other organ damage as well as stomach disorders, blood poisoning and cancers.

Absorption – contaminants can be absorbed into the skin, bloodstream, bone marrow and organs of the body.   This can occur during radiation exposures or result from exposure in other ways such as *contact*.   Toxins that accumulate in the body can block natural functions such as blood cell manufacturing, the oxygen carrying capacity of blood, proper functioning of the nervous system and organ failure.

Contact – certain pollutants can cause surface irritation, burns, swelling, and even freezing of skin and eyes.   Most exposures such as these are short term since the effects are usually immediate and readily apparent, and the affected person will try to stop the exposure.   The additional route of *absorption* can often be a concern after a contact exposure.

Assessing the risk associated with a contaminant means evaluating the possible exposure routes and the reasonable duration of exposure. Furthermore, the potentially adverse health effects of contaminants are directly related to how toxic the contaminants are and the ways they get into the body.

Of special concern is the exposure of infants and children to environmental toxins.   Because of their age and rapidly developing organs and nervous systems, infants and young children are highly susceptible to the toxic effects of pollutants. Greater apprehension is also focused on the young because diseases have the opportunity to develop over ten, twenty, or even thirty years.

HOME EXPOSURES

In your home, exposures to environmental hazards can occur through all of the possible routes. Contaminants may remain in surface soil after an oil spill, or contaminants may migrate in surface water. Both of these situations can represent a potential contact hazard. Metal pollutants such as arsenic, mercury, lead, zinc and cadmium, for example, can persist for long periods in building materials, soil and water. The contaminants can be present in a home and yard because of past industrial use of a structure and property, or because of the placement of contaminated fill materials that were imported during property development. A family may end up suffering exposures by breathing and ingesting airborne dusts and vapors or by gardening and other simple yard use.

Other home exposure risks, such as those resulting from inhalation, are generally related to the potential for radon, the volatility of a contaminant substance such as gasoline, or the ease with which contaminant material becomes airborne. Air quality problems can develop in a home because pollutants migrate in gases, particulates, fumes and vapor form. The migration results by seeping through floor slabs, along utility lines and even by being dissolved into the water supply.

The ingestion of pollutants in a home environment most often occurs through consuming water with low levels of organic or inorganic contaminants. Without knowledge of the almost infinite number of potential sources, we may never have reason to suspect that our drinking water can be easily contaminated by a whole host of both natural and man-made pollutants. It is often found that this type of exposure happens over extended periods because the contaminants may be at extremely low levels, and therefore, go unnoticed. One of the most common examples of the ingestion of a pollutant at low concentrations over time, is lead in drinking water or lead contaminated dust originating from paint in the home.

DELAYED OR IMMEDIATE

Exposure to environmental hazards may cause an effect that is delayed or immediate. A delayed response can occur such as when low level carcinogens (cancer causing agents) exist in a drinking water supply. In these cases, years of constant exposure to even minute concentrations may eventually produce a significant adverse effect.

Whether caused by short-term or long-term exposures, most cancers take years to develop. Because of this latency period, and because lifestyles change, and people relocate, it is often difficult to determine the exact cause of health problems. Although higher rates of disease may be identified in a geographic area, it is necessary to examine carefully the complete history of the affected individuals to assess possible causes. Unfortunately, the causes often remain mysteries for years.

A notorious example of a contamination detective case occurred in Woburn, Massachusetts. Some of the groundwater supply wells for the municipality of Woburn were removed from service in 1979 after illegal dumping raised concerns about potential contamination of the wells. Laboratory tests ultimately revealed industrial solvents in the water supply. Families in the area believed the solvent originated from wastes dumped by a number of nearby manufacturers.

Despite the fact that residents had been complaining for years about the odor and taste of their water, the contamination of the water supply may not have been discovered had the dumping incident not occurred. Studies of Woburn citizens indicated increased rates of leukemia and other health problems. Extensive court battles ensued between residents seeking accountability and the suspected manufacturing facilities that eventually admitted to long histories of indiscriminate waste discharges. The case ultimately became the subject of a best-selling book and the movie - *"A Civil Action"*.

AN IMMEDIATE TOXIC DISASTER

Hazardous material exposures may also cause more immediate adverse health effects. In these cases, there is generally little doubt as to the cause. A drastic example of an immediate cause and effect, as well as an example of risks due to residential/industrial intermingling, happened in 1984 near Bhopal, India.

Over many years, the local population grew and expanded small shantytowns virtually to the boundaries of a Union Carbide Corporation-owned pesticide manufacturing facility. Late one night in December, as safety measures failed, a lethal gas began escaping from partially underground storage tanks at the plant. The gas formed as a low-lying fog that rapidly spread over dozens of square miles. Thousands of people and animals were killed almost immediately and tens of thousands more suffered serious injuries such as blindness, convulsions, emphysema and still births.

Despite safety precautions, backup systems, alarms, and vain as well as valiant attempts to stop the release, the accident happened. You might think, however, that such a disaster could never happen in the United States. You would be wrong.

Union Carbide Corporation was quickly criticized for cutting safety corners due to more relaxed regulations in a country desperate for foreign investments. In defense of the safety measures Union Carbide had in India, the U.S. chairman of the corporation, Warren M. Anderson, said, "our safety standards in the U.S. are identical to those in India or Brazil or some place else. Same equipment, same design, same everything."

While this statement may have been an attempt to bolster the argument that the foreign safety measures were no less vigilant, it raised the unintended comparison that "same" means the disaster could just as easily have happened in the United States.

THE AIR WE BREATHE

Airborne contaminants, commonly found in the home and the surrounding environment, can be responsible for causing numerous ailments and even deaths. The air we breathe frequently includes pollutants such as carbon monoxide, ozone, hydrocarbons, particulate matter and radon. Smog and other types of air pollution contribute to malignancies and respiratory problems such as asthma, bronchitis and emphysema. Radon, a naturally occurring radioactive gas, is found at unacceptable levels in a large percentage of U.S. homes and is estimated to cause thousands of lung cancer deaths per year. This death rate is second only to the number of deaths attributed to smoking.

THE WATER WE DRINK

Public and private drinking water systems can be readily impacted by contaminants that seep into groundwater or surface water supplies. Pollutants also have the ability to find their way into water treatment and distribution systems. Regional groundwater contamination, due to industrial discharges, is often responsible for shutting down entire public water systems. In those cases where the water supply can not be terminated, adding extensive treatment processes is often required. In many treatment systems, chlorination of water supplies is performed to address bacteriological concerns. Ironically though, the addition of chlorine in the treatment process can drastically increase the toxicity of cancer-causing chemicals that may already exist in the water supply.

"ACCEPTABLE" LEVELS

As technology has improved, we have been able to detect contaminants in soil, water, and in air at increasingly lower levels. At the same time, this technology has enabled scientists to identify that for some contaminants, significant impacts to our health can occur at even minute concentrations.

Consequently, the EPA and individual states establish limits for many common contaminants in drinking water.

Acceptable levels for contaminants, that humans may consume, are often as low or lower than one microgram per liter (one part per billion). This is an extremely small percentage. For example, one part per billion, when we compare it to time, is the equivalent of only one day in almost three million years. The drinking water standard for benzene (a common industrial organic chemical and component in gasoline) is only one part per billion. At this concentration, just one fluid ounce of benzene could contaminate enough drinking water to fill a swimming pool that is ten feet deep by twenty feet wide by one mile long!

In most cases, the acceptable contaminant exposure levels have been determined through laboratory studies of animals. Unfortunately, this approach is less than perfect because questions always exist about whether a health effect can be directly extrapolated from animals to humans (not to mention the fact that the animals are never too keen about the testing). Toxicological studies must also try to answer issues of whether the exposure concentrations, and the rates that are simulated in the laboratory, are realistic representations of typical life exposures.

In situations where human data are available - as a result of controlled studies, investigations of accidental poisonings, or examination of disease clusters - the study groups are often so small that the potential for other influencing factors is difficult to evaluate. Among other factors, human toxicological studies must take into account geographic variations, migration rates and cultural differences. For example, if a disease rate were found to be higher in one region versus another, the suggestion would be that there is a differing exposure to some environmental factor. However, consideration must also be given towards genetic and lifestyle variations that may exist as a result of cultural migrations. For these reasons, a cause and effect can be difficult to prove.

RISK VERSUS BENEFIT

Everyday of our lives we consciously and unconsciously evaluate risks while simultaneously weighing the benefits derived from a certain way of living. Driving a car down the street involves some risk - using the car to visit the dentist may involve even more risk. Alternatively, having the teeth necessary to chew a meal (after driving to a favorite restaurant) has its benefits.

With environmental hazards, some risks are involuntarily thrust upon us. In other circumstances, we choose to accept or reject the risks. When we consider accepting a risk, the decision making process must ask whether a risk has been fully identified, whether it may be an occupational risk, whether the effect of exposure is immediate or delayed, and even whether the effect is reversible.

In our homes and communities, hazards will always exist. They will change as the environment goes through transitions, and new risks may develop. As individuals, we may decide that the benefits of living in a certain home or in a certain community outweigh the risks. Alternatively, once risks are defined, we may take measures to reduce or eliminate the risks.

NO FREE LUNCH

Eliminating risk is usually an expensive proposition. The cost of a clean environment can be high. If we want to ensure that the hazardous wastes we produce do not present a future risk to our drinking water supplies, then we must be prepared to build and pay for expensive, modern sanitary landfills, incinerators or other treatment facilities.

If we do not want waste disposal and treatment sites in our "backyards", then we must be prepared to pay more for the transportation to and disposal of the waste in someone else's backyard. Wars of NIMBY (not in my backyard) are constantly raging among the public and the generators (often the same), and between communities, states and the federal government. The waste we produce has to go somewhere. In attempts to maintain public safety and minimize risk, increasingly strict environmental regulations on industry, commercial facilities, and even governmental sites, means the cost for compliance rises. Of course, the costs are then typically passed on to the public.

Consider Key West, Florida. Over the past twenty years, increasing development and tourism resulted in serious wastewater handling and treatment problems, as well as solid-waste disposal problems. As a tourist spot and home for year-round residents, these concerns threatened the very livelihood of the community. Building new and better waste management facilities became necessary to preserve environmental safety. Ironically, the costs of the new facilities increased utility rates so high that the cost of living became prohibitive for many of the long-time residents.

It often becomes necessary to take legal action against polluters to force them to cease an activity or to compel the cleanup of an environmental problem. It is hard and expensive to investigate and prove environmental contamination. In addition, it is harder still to prove damages as the issues of long-term impacts can be difficult to determine. A contamination case can be further complicated by arguments over whether a polluter serves a greater good while a few individuals are hurt. This can be the situation when a polluting industry is the only major employer or the primary tax base in a community. Forcing an expensive cleanup can put the industry, and therefore, the town out of business.

SAFE, SORRY, OR IGNORANT?

Environmental hazards and risks that are clearly identified are rare. Does spending enormous amounts of money to address potential risks make sense, or is the money better spent on hazards proven to cause disease? Is it much ado about nothing or is it always better to be safe than sorry? All too often emotions are involved. Fear of the unknown causes irrational decisions. Of course, it is difficult not to be emotional when the health of your family is involved.

Proper perspective must be maintained. It does not make sense to spend millions of dollars to ensure that no asbestos materials remain in schools, if we do not put the same effort into ensuring that when children go to bed at night there are working smoke alarms in all homes. It is a fear of the unknown that often drives emotional bad decisions rather than common sense good ones.

Concerns about environmental hazards need to be based in reality – fact and science. We must be informed to allow a rational evaluation of risk, to make a valid decision on whether the risk is acceptable and to learn what is available to mitigate the risk. Too often hysteria, half-truths, and misunderstandings result in virtually baseless fears that do more harm than good. Do we understand the true risk?

DIHYDROGEN MONOXIDE

The issue of informed decisions is easily represented by the example of dihydrogen monoxide – an often deadly chemical compound that requires governmental controls and regulations. Despite this, the compound remains in widespread use throughout the United States. It is extensively used as an industrial solvent and as a component in chemical manufacturing operations. It is also used as a fire retardant and to spread pesticides and herbicides. The problem is that tens of thousands of people are killed each year by dihydrogen monoxide.

Dihydrogen monoxide routinely leaks from faulty valves, pipelines, underground storage tanks, and unlined lagoons where the discharges can enter surface water and groundwater. Because of the improper storage and often indiscriminant use of dihydrogen monoxide, laboratory analyses of samples can regularly identify the compound in water supplies throughout the United States. Human exposure can occur through contact, ingestion and inhalation. Exposure can cause nausea, skin deformities, profuse sweating and even suffocation. The compound has also been identified in the bodies of terminal patients and those with neurological diseases.

Despite the proven health risks associated with dihydrogen monoxide, it has not been regulated out of existence. In fact, it remains an invasive compound in our lives. What should be done? Because we know the definite hazards associated with it, should it be banned now? Is more governmental oversight necessary and should we be satisfied with whatever precautions eventually regulate exposures? Are more studies appropriate or should we act now, ban it, and be safe rather than sorry?

Maybe it is not as bad as it sounds. Maybe without dihydrogen monoxide, life as we know it would be impossible. Maybe it is not a terrible sounding chemical, but instead a vital part of life.

Dihydrogen monoxide is also known by the chemical formula H_2O – or even better known as plain water. What we do not know sometimes allows us to make incorrect assumptions, rather than to make sure we fully understand the issues involved.

ELECTROMAGNETIC FIELDS

Since the early 1980's, the issue of electromagnetic fields, and potential adverse health effects, has been extensively studied here and abroad. The issue is cause for a substantial level of concern in many people. Despite the numerous studies, no conclusive findings have yet formed the basis for uniform public decisions or action.

Electromagnetic fields are generated by appliances and electrical transmission wires. Concern has existed for quite some time that the fields generated could cause ailments including childhood leukemia and birth defects. These concerns have even similarly extended to cellular telephones and satellite transmissions. Vernon, New Jersey has a cluster of Down's Syndrome cases and a high concentration of satellite transmitting stations. Questions have been raised as to whether the transmitters could be causing the disorders.

While some studies indicate a link between electromagnetic fields and health effects, others have failed to establish one. There is some question as to how human cells could be impacted and many researchers agree that most fields are relatively low. As a result, the public's level of concern varies. Just as some families may be deciding to move away from homes close to electrical transmission lines, heavy development often has new neighborhoods being constructed even closer. Due to the concerns over the potential hazards, some utility companies have been forced to reroute lines and some states have established allowable limits for field strengths. However, the final verdict is not yet in.

The issue becomes a personal one. If a risk is presented by transmission lines, how big is the risk? Is it small enough to be acceptable or even negligible? The question may be answered by field strengths and proximity to the source. With respect to these factors, it is likely that the fields generated by home appliances such as heating blankets, computer terminals, and maybe even clock radios could represent a higher exposure. In everyday use, we are certainly much closer to these appliances than to overhead transmission lines.

Once again, we face a situation that we just do not know for sure and perhaps it is better to err on the side of caution. If proximity were proven to be a major factor in determining the hazard, it would seem that avoidance would be the key to minimizing risk. Even without a final verdict, you can take some simple and inexpensive steps to minimize the potential for risk. Put your child's bedroom, for example, furthest in the home from the transmission line. Place a clock radio at the foot of the bed rather than at the head. Avoid excessive use of heating blankets. These are personal issues that may not have final answers for some time.

RADON

"Safe upon the solid rock the ugly houses stand: Come and see my shining
palace built upon the sand!"

Edna St. Vincent Millay

WHAT IT IS

Seven to thirty thousand-lung cancer deaths per year – that is how many
the Environmental Protection Agency (EPA) estimates are caused by
radon. The rate of death is second only to the rate caused by smoking.

Radon is a radioactive gas that originates from natural materials in the earth.
Because it is a gas, it can migrate into and accumulate in homes - usually
under conditions that can readily occur in most houses.

Under the correct, but not rare, circumstances, radon gas can accumulate to
levels that increase the risk of cancer. Despite this, the public appears less
attentive and concerned about radon issues. This lack of concern may be due
in part to the fact that in almost all cases radon originates from unseen natural

sources, rather than from a more ominous entity such as a nuclear power plant or a spill from a chemical manufacturing facility.

Radon is a tasteless, odorless and colorless gas formed by the normal decay of radioactive Uranium-238, which exists within various types of soil and rock that make up the crust of the earth. In general, areas of land underlain by coarse sediments and sandstone bedrock will have lower concentrations of radon than areas that have thin soils and are underlain by relatively shallow shale or granite bedrock. Recognize, however, that even within small geographic areas, geology varies significantly, and so to do the levels of radon that can potentially develop.

Inasmuch as the half-life (time that it takes for one-half of a radioactive substance to decay) of radon is short, in order for significant concentrations to reach the surface, the gas needs to migrate along relatively permeable pathways. Upon nearing the surface, the gas may have the opportunity to migrate into homes. Despite the short half-life, areas of fractured rock can facilitate the upward migration of radon for hundreds of feet. As radon gas forms, it migrates to the surface and is released into the atmosphere where the EPA estimates it is responsible for approximately half of all natural background radiation.

A GAS WITH A PAST

For hundreds of years, it had been suspected that miners were exposed to an unseen, underground hazard that resulted in lung cancer, although there was no way of knowing the cause. By the early part of the twentieth century, it was known that radiation could destroy cells. It was believed therefore, that drinking water with dissolved radium in it could cure cancers and other ailments. Of course, this thinking did not consider the impact that the radiation would have on healthy cells.

From the turn of the century until approximately the 1930s, a large number of devices were marketed to dissolve radium into drinking water. Many mines were converted into underground spas, becoming popular locations to inhale radon gas and drink tainted water. Fortunately, the popularity of such practices dropped off when the number of prominent people who regularly consumed radium also dropped off – dead.

The hazard of radium was also highlighted in the 1920s. It was then that a considerable number of women, who painted luminous watch dials in a New Jersey factory, contracted various cancers. At the time, it was a common practice to sharpen the point of the paintbrush by licking it. The problem was that the watch dials were being painted with radium to make them glow in the dark.

MODERN CONCERNS

Only over the past ten to fifteen years, however, has it been more commonly recognized that radon gas can accumulate to unacceptable levels in the home and create a significant health risk for a much larger number of people. As a radioactive material, radon decays to "daughter" products. This process results in the release of energy and mass. In the course of decay, minute radioactive particles are emitted, which can be inhaled to possibly lodge in the lungs. Alpha, beta, and/or gamma radiation can be emitted from the particles during the decay series, resulting in cell damage that can ultimately lead to lung cancer.

Due to dispersion into the atmosphere, the levels of radon that we breathe in the exterior air are extremely low. Average outdoor concentrations are estimated to range between 0.2 and 0.4 picocuries per liter of air (pCi/L - a picocurie is one trillionth of a curie - which is a measure of radioactive decay). The average, interior radon concentration in United States homes ranges between approximately 1 to 1.5 pCi/L.

Radon concentrations greater than 4 pCi/L are considered unacceptable and the EPA recommends corrective measures to reduce the levels. In fact, because of the presence of even small risks, the EPA suggests taking steps to reduce radon concentrations as much as possible even if the levels are already below 4 pCI/L. Any reduction, the EPA reasons, can only be beneficial. The benefits derived from further decreases however, must be weighed against the costs associated with the reduction measures.

"A NUCLEAR ACCIDENT"

In an ironic set of circumstances, we can thank the nuclear industry for the somewhat accidental discovery of the hazard associated with radon infiltrating into and accumulating in homes. In 1984, as the Limerick Nuclear Power Plant was preparing to go on-line in Pottstown, Pennsylvania, routine radiation monitoring of workers identified an individual who regularly triggered the alarms. Although alarms are generally unusual, this was particularly so because the worker triggered the alarms on his way *into* the plant.

Investigations at the plant revealed no known source for the radiation exposure. It was not until the worker's home in nearby Boyertown, Pennsylvania was studied, that it was determined that his home was exposing him to more hazardous levels of radiation than his place of work - a nuclear power plant! Monitoring in the worker's home detected an astonishing radon level of 2,700 pCi/L, which was causing a significant exposure to radiation for the entire family. As an example of how variable radon levels can be, although other homes in the area also had elevated levels, the radon concentration in the house next door to the worker's was less than 1 pCi/L.

GEOGRAPHIC VARIATIONS

U.S. Department of Energy and EPA studies have produced estimates that between six and almost ten percent of American homes have radon concentrations that exceed 4 pCi/L. Higher than normal concentrations have been found in at least thirty states amounting to an estimated seven to eight million homes. Figure 4.1 is a map that is a general representation of average potential indoor radon concentrations across the United States. Due to the possibility for wide variations within small geographic areas, testing of individual homes should be conducted if there are any concerns about radon.

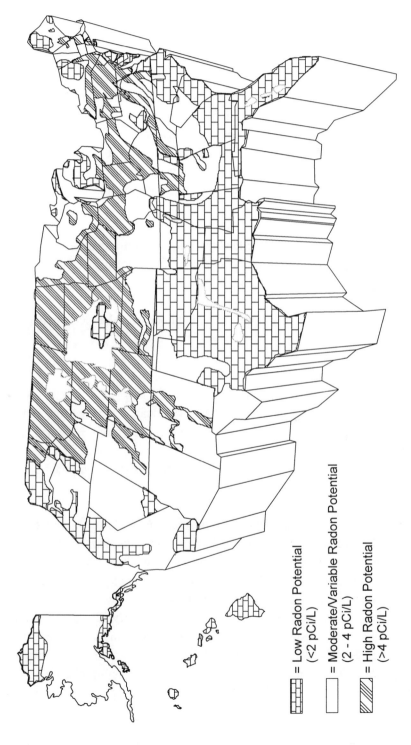

FIGURE 4.1 - GENERALIZED MAP OF RADON POTENTIAL (Based on U.S.G.S. data 1995)

GEOLOGY

In almost all cases, the source for elevated levels of radon in the home is the natural decay of uranium within soil and rock. Geologic materials contain variable quantities of uranium, and therefore, the potential for occurrence of radon differs as much as the underlying geology. The ease of upward migration and dispersion depends in part on the types of soil. Furthermore, variable structures within bedrock formations, such as fractures and faults, can create connected voids that will significantly enhance the upward migration of radon.

In general, areas that are underlain by igneous and metamorphic rock will have a higher likelihood of radon occurrence. Locations characterized by thick sediments, such as those found in many coastal areas, generally have a lower potential for radon accumulation. Figure 4.2 is a generalized geologic cross section that illustrates the relative likelihood of radon occurrence.

NOT ALWAYS NATURAL

Aside from natural geologic causes, radon gas can originate from industrial and mining wastes as well as from building materials such as stone that may contain uranium. Unfortunately, there have been a number of cases across the country where homes have been built on fill material that was contaminated with uranium.

In three neighboring communities in northern New Jersey, more than 300 residential properties were constructed on or near radium waste disposal sites. It was suspected that the radioactive waste was disposed of from radium processing facilities, which operated nearby in the early 1900s. The waste contaminated soil had been used as a fill material for low lying areas and had also been mixed with other materials for sidewalk and foundation construction. The result - a nightmare. Beginning in the mid-1980s, high levels of radon gas were identified in dozens of homes. For the next fifteen years, home after home was treated under one collective cleanup program with the installation of radon mitigation systems and in many cases the

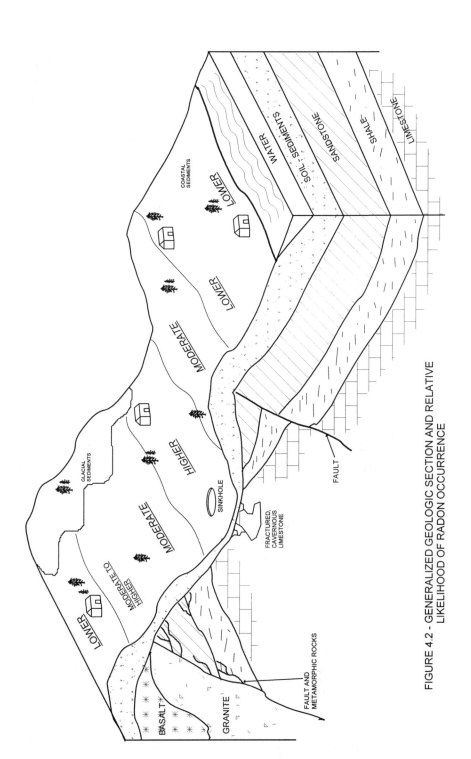

FIGURE 4.2 - GENERALIZED GEOLOGIC SECTION AND RELATIVE
LIKELIHOOD OF RADON OCCURRENCE

excavation of entire properties. Similar circumstances have occurred in Colorado, where mining tailings were also used as backfill around homes and in New York, where rock that contained uranium had been used as construction material.

THE HEALTH RISK

Innumerable studies have shown that a non-smoker, who is regularly exposed to radon levels higher than 4 pCi/L, has a 0.2% to a 1.0% chance of developing lung cancer over a lifetime of exposure. Radon has been identified as a definite human carcinogen and the risk of lung cancer is directly proportional to the concentration that accumulates in the home and the duration of exposure. As is the case with many environmental contaminants, due to developing or perhaps weaker respiratory systems, the young and the elderly are more susceptible to the effects of radon.

Although living in a home with greater than a 4 pCi/L radon level increases the risk of dying from lung cancer, you must consider whether the levels are consistently elevated. Attention should also be paid as to where in the home the exposure to high concentrations occurs. Radon levels change significantly with the seasons and vary considerably throughout a house, so exposures correspondingly fluctuate. It is up to the homeowner to evaluate a house and their family's lifestyles to determine what their exposure could be and what level of risk is acceptable.

ANOTHER REASON NOT TO SMOKE

An individual's smoking history also influences greatly the risk of lung cancer from radon. A smoker increases his or her risk of radon induced lung cancer by approximately 10 to 15 times. By breathing in smoke, either first or secondhand, it provides an additional mechanism for radon to enter the lungs. Table 4.1 details EPA data on the relative risks associated with various radon levels and a comparison with other health risks and lifestyles.

Table 4.1 - Radon Exposures and Relative Risk

Radon Level (pCi/L)	Lifetime exposure and number of lung cancers out of 1,000 people	Relative Risk	Recommended Action (stop smoking and...)
20	**non-smokers** - about 8 **smokers** - about 135	Compares to risk of violent crime death. 100 times risk of drowning.	Mitigate levels
10	**non-smokers** - about 4 **smokers** - about 71	100 times the risk of dying in a home fire.	Mitigate levels
8	**non-smokers** - about 3 **smokers** - about 57	10 times the risk of dying in a plane crash.	Mitigate levels
4	**non-smokers** - about 2 **smokers** - about 29	Compares to the risk of drowning. 100 times the risk of dying in a plane crash	Mitigate levels
2	**non-smokers** - about 1 **smokers** - about 15	Compares to the risk of dying in a home fire. 2 times the risk of dying in a car crash.	Consider action.
1.3	**non-smokers** - about 1 **smokers** - about 9	Average indoor radon level.	Difficult to mitigate below this level.
0.4	**non-smokers** - about 1 **smokers** - about 3	Average outdoor radon level	Difficult to mitigate below this level.

Source: Adapted from USEPA, 1998.

MODUS OPERANDI

Because of simple physical properties, radon gas can enter a home from the underlying and surrounding soil. The interior of a home, especially during the winter, is typically at a lower air pressure than the pressure that exists in the surrounding ground. Because of this pressure differential, radon gas that is migrating through the voids in soil and rock will move from the zone of higher pressure into the zone of lower pressure – a home. This problem is made worse in the colder months due to reduced ventilation and the use of heaters, dryers, fireplaces and other combustion devices that use internal air and further lower the pressure in a home.

Radon typically enters a dwelling through basement walls and floor slabs or any portion of a building that is in direct contact with the surrounding soil. It can also enter a home through sumps, utility service lines, or by contaminating the groundwater that is drawn into household supply wells. Radon that enters a home in well water can expose people through a number of pathways, e.g. cooking, bathing, washing clothes or other uses which would allow the release of the gas into the surrounding interior air. Figure 4.3 illustrates the most common migration pathways that potentially allow radon to get into a home.

Drinking water that is contaminated with low levels of radon is probably not a significant health risk because the gas is not inhaled into the lungs. More of a risk likely occurs as the water aerates during the process of taking it from the tap. If the water supply to a home comes from surface water sources there is generally no concern associated with radon in household water. This is because the accumulation of radon in surface water is not common; the gas can vent directly to the atmosphere.

The ability for radon to concentrate can also be a function of changes in weather factors such as atmospheric pressure, temperature and precipitation. And remember, differences in geology and building construction can cause wide radon variations in a small geographical area. The presence or absence of radon in a neighbor's home should not be taken as an indication of the levels in your own home.

MEASURES TO CONSIDER

The EPA recommends radon testing for all residences with living areas below the third-floor level. In the majority of cases, radon levels in a basement or the lowest level of a home are higher than in other areas of a

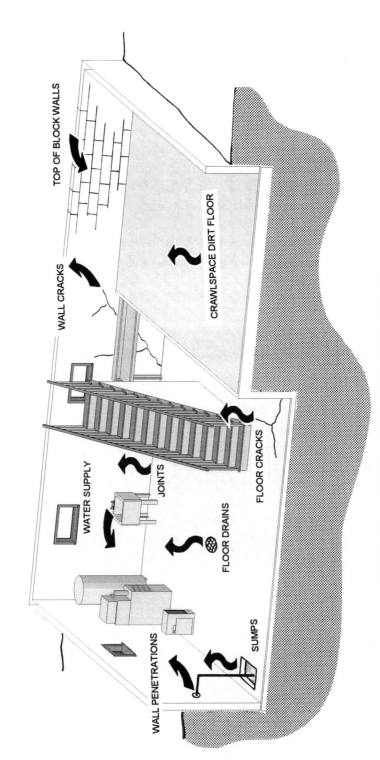

FIGURE 4.3 - COMMON RADON INFILTRATION ROUTES

home. This is because the radon concentration dilutes by escaping the house through vents, windows and doors as it migrates upward. Testing of basements should be conducted because they represent moderate use areas in many, if not most homes. Testing crawl spaces is seldom warranted because they are not used for living space. Results from a crawl space, however, can be used to represent potential worst case conditions and to measure and evaluate the reduction in concentrations for living areas above a crawl space. Figure 4.4 illustrates the general variability in radon potential with respect to home location and construction.

How much you use affected areas must be considered when you assess the risk associated with radon. For example, a basement that is used for nothing other than storage and perhaps laundry/utilities would obviously pose less of a risk than a basement with a recreation room and a comparable radon level. Aside from considering the regularity of room use, a homeowner should take into account the ages of the people who live in the home. When there is a known or suspected problem, obviously it is not advisable to place a child's bedroom on a lower level or to use a basement for a playroom.

TESTING AND EVALUATION

If you are in the market for a home, conduct at least one radon test. Depending on the findings, additional testing may be warranted. Many localities now require at least one radon test before issuing a certificate of occupancy. Self-test kits are available or professional testing companies can be hired to do the testing. When concerns exist about the possibility of radon in well water, a professional should be used due to the more complex nature of the sampling procedure.

Testing for radon in the air in your own (or a prospective home) can be done by purchasing relatively inexpensive sensor kits at home supply stores or through mail order. These sensors are often the same as those used by professionals and usually cost less than $25 to $30, including the charge for analysis by mail. Short-term kits are the cheapest and are generally set in the area of concern for a period of 2 to 7 days before being submitted

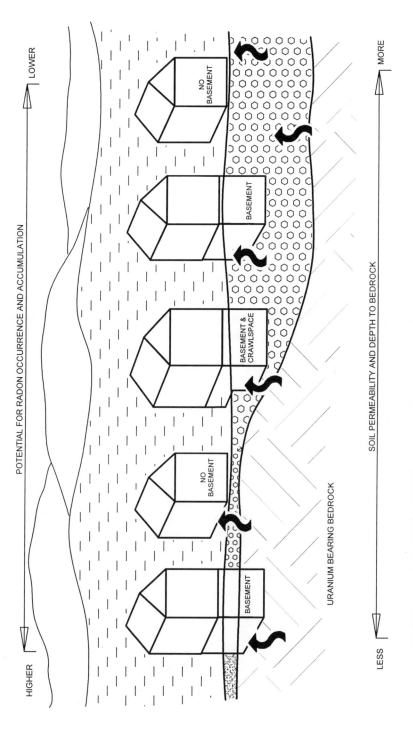

FIGURE 4.4 - RADON ACCUMULATION VARIABILITY VERSUS HOME LOCATION AND CONSTRUCTION

for analysis. Long-term kits are exposed for at least 90 days. A longer test period is typically more representative of the true conditions; abnormal highs and lows will be averaged out by measuring the radon concentrations over a range of weather conditions and household use patterns.

A general correlation can be made between using the results from air monitoring sensors and the potential for radon in a household water supply that comes from a well. Under situations where radon concentrations are non-detectable in the home over an extended time, it is generally reasonable to assume that unsafe levels of radon gas are not normally emanating from the water supply.

While a home may not be present on an undeveloped property, the potential for radon occurrence can still be investigated. In these cases, a sensor can be buried in the ground, at least a few feet deep, and subsequently tested. Depending upon the results, you can then decide what degree of radon resistant home construction or removal system may be warranted.

Unfortunately, the time is typically not available to conduct long-term testing when you are buying a home or property. However, real estate sales agreements can include contingency clauses, related to radon, that allow a buyer to back out of the contract if testing shows unsatisfactory results. The following table summarizes EPA recommendations for significantly elevated radon levels and the corresponding period in which action should be taken.

Table 4.2 - EPA Recommendations for Radon Mitigation based on Detected Levels

Radon Level (pCi/L)	Action
4-20	Mitigate within 1-2 years
20-200	Mitigate within several months
>200	Within one month increase ventilation, consider relocation during mitigation measures.

Source: Adapted from USEPA, 1998

HONESTY – THE BEST POLICY

If a seller is responsible for conducting the testing for radon, it is important to scrutinize the procedures. If possible, visit the house at various times during the testing period to ensure that excessive ventilation is not occurring. Unfortunately, it is not uncommon for a homeowner with a radon problem to leave every window open during the testing period in an effort to artificially lower the results. When feasible, conduct the testing during colder months. The homeowner would be less likely to ventilate the home during cold weather and the results would be more representative of worst-case conditions.

Simple devices are available to ensure that tampering with the testing sensor does not occur. These devices will prevent the test sensor from being relocated within the house, simply placed outside until the test period is over, or even replaced with a fresh sensor near the end of the testing period. Anti-tampering measures include specialized tape to secure the sensor as well as cases that lock the sensor in place.

CONSTRUCTION ASSESSMENT

Aside from variations in geology, the degree to which radon may find its way into a home, and the degree to which it may concentrate, is related to the type of home construction and the amount of ventilation that occurs. As our homes have become increasingly "tight" and energy-efficient with improved construction methods, sealants, and better windows, the potential for radon to accumulate is enhanced. This is one case where a big, old, drafty house may be a good thing.

In some cases, if the entry of radon into a home can be shown to be the result of structural defects, the builder can be held responsible for damages, including the increased cancer risk. Builders also can be held liable if they have built a home in a known radon problem area, but did not take measures to notify the homeowner or to build with techniques that can mitigate the problem.

Consequently, in areas where radon accumulation is considered to be a reasonable possibility, radon resistant building methods are becoming standard. Many builders are automatically including the basic components of a venting system during the construction. The system can be activated later if unacceptable radon levels are detected in future testing. In almost all circumstances, it is significantly cheaper to install the radon reduction components during house construction rather than after the fact.

Options also include wiring for a fan system if accelerated venting becomes necessary. Figure 4.5 illustrates a generalized mitigation system and simple radon resistant construction materials.

MITIGATION

Uncomplicated, effective, and relatively inexpensive measures are available to significantly reduce elevated radon concentrations in a home. The available measures fall into one of two categories. Either the amount of radon that enters a home can be reduced in the first place, or the radon can be expelled once it has entered.

PREVENT

In some situations applying sealers to cracks and voids in and around a floor slab and walls may sufficiently reduce radon infiltration. Unfortunately, this process is seldom completely effective unless all entry points are identified and blocked and every crack, including minute ones, is fully sealed.

Attention should also be paid to voids around utility pipes and basement windows. Floor sumps should be covered and sealed with caulk around the edges, and sealant should be applied around any piping that penetrates the floor or foundation. In addition, hollow block walls, typical of many foundations, can allow migration upward to the house sill. The use of a solid, poured foundation can eliminate this avenue of exposure.

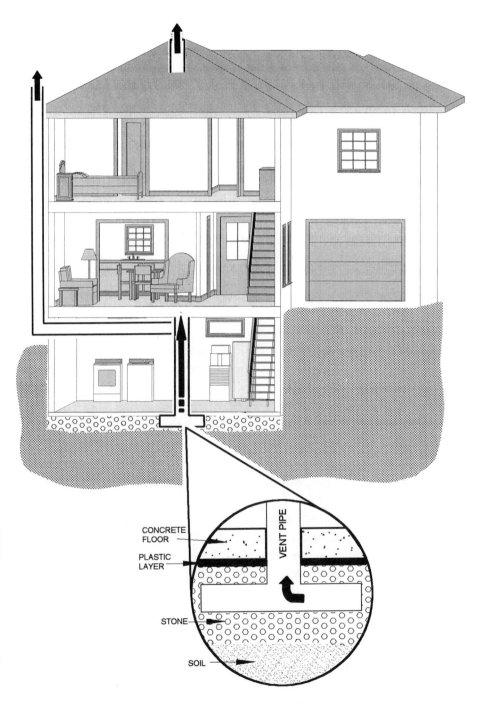

FIGURE 4.5 - PASSIVE RADON REDUCTION SYSTEM

REMOVE

Because radon is a gas, other mitigation measures can readily take advantage of its physical properties and mobility. Systems can be installed around the exterior of the foundation to reduce the air pressure in the soil. This pressure reduction can induce radon in the earth to take the path of least resistance, remain in the soil, and exit at the exterior ground surface and disperse into the atmosphere.

Other radon reduction systems may consist of sub-slab and in-house venting or fan systems that remove the gas and vent interior concentrations directly to the exterior. This type of ventilation may reduce concentrations, but by exhausting interior air/radon to the exterior, it may be inadvertently lowering the interior pressure and actually encouraging additional radon migration into the interior.

A better and more efficient approach is to create a venting system beneath or around the slab that is connected via piping directly to the exterior, usually above the roofline. The pressure beneath the slab will be lowered and the radon will then continue to follow the path of least resistance. To improve the venting effectiveness, the piping is often augmented with a fan system to accelerate flow to the exterior.

In more temperate climates, where heating costs are reduced, dilution can be the solution. Exterior air (with naturally lower radon concentrations) can be forced into the interior to dilute the radon levels. Done right, these measures can generally reduce radon concentrations by as much as 99%. In most cases, the costs for mitigation are less than $2,000. Installation of system components during construction typically adds less than $1,000 to $2,000 to construction costs.

With respect to the treatment of radon contaminated well water, the options are relatively limited, but effective. Commonly, treatment consists of a simple gas stripping system, which passes air through the contaminated water and removes the radon gas. Dissolved radon can also be eliminated from water by using granular activated carbon filters. Either of these systems would best be deployed by treating the entire water supply at the point of entry into the home. Individual systems at each faucet, washing machine, shower, etc., would not be practical.

LEAD

"Iron rusts from disuse; stagnant water loses its
purity and in cold weather becomes frozen; even so
does inaction sap the vigor of the mind."

Leonardo da Vinci

HEAVY METAL

L ead is a dense, silver–gray metal that is soft and malleable. Because
of these properties, for more than a thousand years, lead has been
incorporated in pottery, piping, coins, paint, utensils and numerous
other items. Lead was also used extensively for pipes and piping connections
in ancient water systems. In fact, the chemical symbol for lead, *Pb*, is derived
from the Latin word for waterworks *"plumbum"* (plumbing).

Unfortunately, lead is highly toxic when ingested (or in some cases inhaled)
over time. It has the tendency to concentrate in the organs and blood, and
high levels of lead can cause nerve damage, birth defects, learning disabilities,
and, in extreme poisoning cases, death. Due to the widespread use of lead in

water systems, utensils, and wine production, it is believed by many that lead poisoning was one of the causes for the fall of ancient Rome.

Present day blood poisoning from lead continues to come from sources including leaded crystal, hobby use, ceramics, and even some imported dishes and processed food containers. The two most common exposure sources for lead that raise the largest concern in the home, are lead-based paint and lead contamination from our drinking water systems.

LEAD-BASED PAINT

For decades, lead was added to household paints because it greatly increased durability. The problem is that dust and paint chips generated from lead-based paint can be ingested (most commonly by children) and eventually result in lead poisoning. This ingestion accounts for the majority of lead poisoning in the home.

Estimates show that approximately 90% of homes that were built before 1940 contain at least some lead paint. According to the United States Department of Housing and Urban Development, this figure drops only to 75% when we consider all private homes built before 1980. This is equivalent to about one-half of all homes in the United States. The occurrence of lead-based paint is greatest in urban areas where the majority of older homes are found. Because settlement of this country occurred from the east to the west, lead-based paint is more common in the older, eastern portions.

1978 BAN

Beginning in 1978, the use of lead-based paint in homes was banned. Unfortunately, leftover stock and "touch-up" paint may have been used for several years after that. Consequently, construction or renovation after 1978 is not a guarantee that lead-based paint is not present in a home.

Lead-based paint was most commonly used on cabinets and to cover trim on doors and windows and other areas that required extra durability. Because these areas are subjected to extensive use and friction from movement and rubbing, the resulting wear and tear accelerates the production of lead-contaminated dust from the paint. Although less common, lead-based paint was also used on walls and ceilings.

When most people think of the hazard and the history associated with lead-based paint, the images brought to mind are those of children eating chips of lead paint. Most commonly though, the exposure occurs in a much more subtle way. Though lead-based paint in the home may not be obviously flaking or peeling, the dust that is naturally generated as the paint ages (chalks) typically contains elevated levels of lead.

Lead-contaminated dust accumulates on all surfaces, including windowsills, tables, toys, and the floor. Of course, children touch all of these things and have a tendency to put their hands and virtually everything else into their mouths – including feet, dropped food, toys, and wet pacifiers. The result is that the lead-contaminated dust is easily ingested and it can then enter the blood stream.

DISCLOSURE OF WHAT IS KNOWN

Because of the hazards associated with lead-based paint, federal regulations went into effect in 1996 (Residential Lead-Based Paint Hazard Reduction Act of 1992). These regulations require landlords and owners of homes built before 1978 to disclose to potential renters and buyers the presence of any known lead-based paint as well as the risks. If lead-based paint is present, the homeowner is not required to remove the paint, but the buyer is permitted to test and consider their options during a 10-day inspection period. The available options may of course include backing out of the sale or price negotiations to cover the cost and inconvenience associated with addressing the paint.

OUTSIDE TOO

Exterior paint also often contains lead. This paint is found on house siding, trim, porches, fences, etc. Flaking or oxidizing lead-based paint either falls or is washed to the ground by rain and snow where it can contaminate the soil around a home. Lead contamination around a home can also occur when exterior structures are sanded or scraped to prepare for repainting, without taking the appropriate precautions to contain the waste paint. Children can then be exposed to the lead by playing in soil near the house as well as by eating food or putting their hands in their mouths without washing first.

Former and present industrial and urban areas, and residential areas built on or near imported backfill materials, are also often found to have elevated lead concentrations in the soil. Lead sources in these areas include lead-based paint in demolition debris, lead used in industrial processes, leaded gasoline emissions, and waste lead-acid batteries. See Chapter 8 for more discussion on soil and contamination from hazardous material sites.

LEAD IN DRINKING WATER

The human body can also absorb lead into blood and organs by consuming water from the tap that is contaminated. For many years, municipal water supply mains were connected to household plumbing systems by lead pipe. Additionally, unless complete plumbing renovations have been conducted, homes built before the first half of the twentieth century often have at least some lead piping within the house. Lead was also used as a component in plumbing solder to reduce the melting point. Unfortunately, until it was banned in 1988, plumbers regularly used lead solder to connect copper piping systems in the home. Like paint, the use of leftover stock after the ban is possible.

Because water is the universal solvent, small amounts of lead from piping and solder leach into a household water supply. The amount of leaching is influenced by the hardness of water and the pH (measurement of acidity). Water that is softer and somewhat acidic will leach more lead than hard or more alkaline water. Expect that the concentrations of lead in the water will correspondingly increase the longer the water remains undisturbed in pipes that include a lead component.

HOT AND COLD

Assuming the source of water supplied to a home is not contaminated with lead, simply running a faucet for a minute or so will greatly reduce possible lead concentrations by purging the water that sat for an extended period. Feeling the water, for a relative temperature change as it is purged, is a good indication that the water, which remained in the pipes (perhaps overnight), has been flushed. Because hotter water has the ability to dissolve more lead than cold water, it is a good practice to use only cold water for drinking and cooking.

Municipal water services can provide information on the content of lead in a public water supply. However, this information cannot answer the question of possible lead contamination that may occur through local service connections outside a house or from household piping that includes lead pipe or lead solder. After the water leaves municipal control, there are no guarantees of quality.

In most cases, the source of lead contamination is associated with the manmade distribution system and not the original water quality. Although relatively rare, lead contamination in private water wells is possible. Chapter 9 provides information on drinking water, private wells, contamination, and treatment options.

The question of water quality, as it relates to lead, becomes most important at the tap. However, lead-based paint is a whole house issue. Figure 5.1 illustrates some of the common locations that lead-based paint and lead in water systems can be found in and around the home.

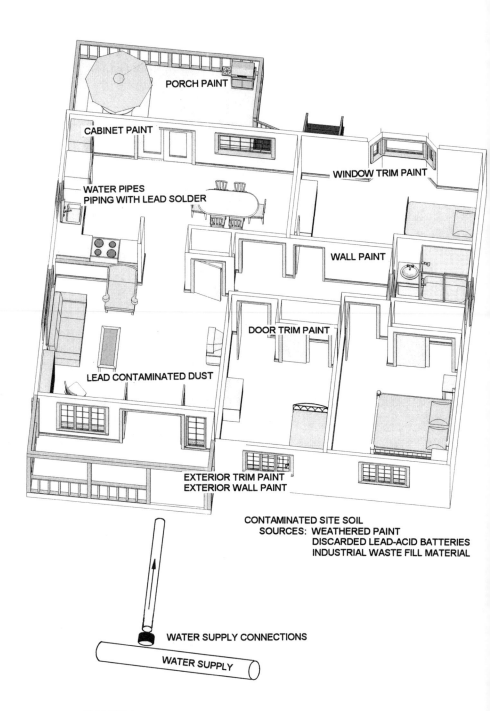

FIGURE 5.1 - LEAD SOURCES IN AND AROUND THE HOME

THE HEALTH RISK

Upon exposure, most commonly through ingestion, the body absorbs lead very slowly. However, the lead is expelled at a much slower rate. Consequently, with continual exposure, this results in an accumulation of lead that will reach toxic levels. Lead will circulate through the body by way of the red blood cells and will concentrate in soft tissue organs like the liver and kidneys. Lead can also be deposited in young bones, where it can be secreted back into the blood stream later in life. As protective cells become damaged, the brain can also become seriously affected.

Early signs of lead poisoning include loss of appetite, weakness, joint pain, high blood pressure, and anemia. Continued poisoning can result in hearing problems, learning disabilities, behavioral problems, neurological damage, growth impairment, kidney and reproductive problems, and lasting brain damage.

BLOOD LEAD LEVELS

According to the Environmental Almanac (1993), a 1992 study in the New England Journal of Medicine, found that blood lead levels in modern humans are on average 1,000 times greater than in our ancestors. In 1960, the Centers for Disease Control set 60 micrograms of lead per deciliter of blood (ug/dl) as the maximum level acceptable for children. Because subsequent studies showed significant adverse effects at substantially lower levels, the threshold was reduced to 25 ug/dl; in 1991, it was reduced again to the current guideline of only 10 ug/dl.

EPA and other governmental studies have shown that above the level of 10 ug/dl, measurable cognitive and behavioral impairment begins. Prompted by numerous findings, that show anywhere from four to sixteen percent of children under the age of five to six have elevated blood lead levels, the federal government has recommended testing all children for lead poisoning by the age of two.

Aside from blood testing, measuring lead contamination in the body can also, and perhaps more accurately, be determined by testing baby teeth or by X-ray techniques. This testing may be warranted because some health professionals believe that much of the lead that is ingested will migrate into bones within months. Depending on the timing, blood testing could give an artificially low indication of the degree of poisoning.

THE YOUNGEST ONES

People of all ages are susceptible to the toxic effects of lead. Adults can endure reproductive and pregnancy problems, high blood pressure, kidney damage, muscular and joint problems, anemia and neurological disorders. However, our greatest concern is focused on fetuses and young children because of a higher likelihood for exposure and because of the heightened susceptibility of the brain and nervous system during early stages of development.

As is the case with many toxins, fetuses can be exposed to lead through a mother's bloodstream. Exposure in the womb results in increased absorption during organ development, and the toxic effects on areas such as the nervous system are heightened. Lead poisoning can also retard growth in pre- and post-natal exposures.

TREATMENT

Fortunately lead poisoning is a treatable condition and most of the harm can be corrected if it is detected early enough. As is the case with some other toxins, lead in the blood can be removed through a medication process called *chelation*. Drug therapy will cause the lead in the bloodstream to precipitate where it can be subsequently eliminated in the urine. Certain medical conditions can be addressed with rehabilitation and therapy, but brain damage from lead poisoning is irreversible.

MONEY MATTERS

While early studies recognized that elevated levels of lead in the blood caused anemia, learning disabilities, and brain damage, malnutrition exacerbates these adverse affects of lead poisoning. Although lead poisoning can be found in all socioeconomic groups, the urban poor (with generally worse nutrition and higher exposures to paint in older buildings) have been especially hard hit.

In the early 1990s, the United States Department of Health and Human Services estimated that 7% of children under the age of six, from medium- to high-income families, might have been subject to lead poisoning. In comparison, the Department estimated that 25% of poor white children and 55% of poor black children may have been afflicted.

Due to increased awareness and prevention, the blood lead levels in children have been dropping over the past twenty years. However, the United States Department of Housing and Urban Development estimates that almost 900,000 children under the age of six continue to have blood lead levels that are too high.

MEASURES TO CONSIDER

The presence of lead-based paint in a home and/or lead in drinking water does not necessarily mean that members of a household will have elevated blood levels. However, if medical screening has identified the poisoning, it is critical to locate and eliminate the source(s) of exposure.

Measures to mitigate the problem may range from simple avoidance to periodic maintenance to complete removal of the lead-based paint. Contaminated water problems may be addressed through flushing, treatment systems, alternative supplies or complete plumbing renovations.

LEAD-BASED PAINT

The primary course of action to avoid and/or reduce the potential for lead poisoning due to paint is to identify the source(s) in the home. If the age of the home is appropriate (pre-1978) or other suspicions exist about the paint quality, testing should be done.

TESTING

Simple screening kits to detect lead in paint and other household items are available in most hardware and home-supply stores. They cost generally less than $3 to $15 per sample. The testing kits are relatively straightforward to use and generally involve applying a lead-sensitive chemical to a paint sample or directly to other suspect surfaces. Although the exact concentration is not defined, a specific color change indicates the presence of lead. More involved mail-order tests involve sending a sample for laboratory analysis to identify the exact percentage of lead in the paint. The current legal limit for lead in paint is 0.06 percent.

More sophisticated home screenings include the professional use of x-ray fluorescence machines. This method produces a relatively quick and complete survey of an entire home.

All assessment methods, whether they entail a screening kit, sample analysis, or the x-ray approach, must take into account the potential for multiple layers of paint that are almost always present in older homes. Although a surface layer of paint may be lead-free, it is important to know for future renovation whether underlying paint layers may be lead-based.

MITIGATION

If you identify lead-based paint, the next step is to assess the condition of the paint and evaluate the potential for exposure and the associated risk. Common sense dictates that lead-based paint on the windowsill of a child's room represents a greater risk than a painted windowsill in a basement that is seldom used. The presence of lead-based paint does not necessarily mean an expensive removal process. Complete removal of all lead-based paint in a home is a permanent and expensive solution, but is seldom necessary and generally should only be considered for homes that have or expect to have young children. If removal is not done, care should be taken to maintain or isolate the paint as discussed below.

In instances where you do decide to remove the paint, the work is best performed by an experienced and qualified contractor. Similar to an asbestos abatement, an improperly conducted lead-based paint removal project could produce dust and conditions that are more hazardous than leaving things alone. A complete abatement can entail either stripping surfaces that are covered with lead-based paint or completely removing and replacing the painted items such as windows, cabinets, trim, and door moldings.

Regulations for private homeowner abatements are less prevalent and stringent than regulations for public housing or rental properties. Paint removal or renovation activities that address lead-based paint should involve careful preparation, protection, and cleanup to minimize the generation of lead dust. Furniture and rooms should be isolated with plastic sheeting. A respirator with filters that will remove lead dust should be worn during the work. Painted surfaces should be wetted before scraping, or a chemical stripper or other lifting agents should be used to reduce the potential for airborne dust. Unless connected to a high efficiency particulate air (HEPA) vacuum, dry sanding is never a good practice; the amount of dust will be drastically increased. All waste material and plastic sheeting should be sealed in multiple plastic bags before proper disposal.

LIVING WITH IT

Other than complete removal, additional options are available to reduce the lead exposure risk. These options are generally simple and significantly less costly, but they do require vigilance and scrupulous cleaning. If you chose to live with the paint, implement a regular program of maintenance and cleaning.

Flaking paint and dust should be removed using a wet method and lead-based paint surfaces should be routinely washed with a trisodium phosphate or phosphate detergent solution to remove accumulations of dust. Towels that are pre-soaked with a high-phosphate solution are available and they work like large, moist toweletes. Unless a HEPA vacuum is used, dry vacuuming of dusty areas is definitely not recommended, because the dust will become airborne and redistributed.

The hazard of lead-based paint is most often mitigated by covering it over with additional coats of paint (non-leaded of course). In some instances, covering lead-based paint with wallpaper, plaster, an additional layer of wallboard, or paneling isolates the risk. If the hazard is painted over or covered, future renovations should take into account the lead-based paint beneath.

EXTERIOR

As with interior paint, deteriorating lead-based paint on or around the exterior of homes can be removed mechanically or chemically. Wear personal respiratory protection and containerize any waste that is generated. Plastic sheeting on the ground and shrubs should be used to prevent spreading paint chips into soil around the house. Lead-based exterior paint can also be addressed by isolating it with new house siding.

LEAD IN DRINKING WATER

Testing for lead in drinking water is typically more involved than testing paint. The most reliable and quantifiable results are obtained by submitting a sample of your water to a qualified analytical laboratory. Analysis costs per sample are usually less than $30 and an exact concentration of lead will be determined. The current EPA action level for lead in drinking water is 15 micrograms per liter (ug/l - parts per billion). This is down from a level of 50 ug/l just a few years ago.

To represent the worst case levels of lead in your water, a sample should be taken directly from the tap after it has sat in the pipes for at least several hours. A good approach is to collect a sample first thing in the morning after the water stood in the pipes overnight. So before you fill the coffeepot, run the water for several seconds and then fill the sample containers supplied by the laboratory.

If laboratory analysis determines that your water is above the EPA guideline for the "first" water out of the tap (15 ug/l), a subsequent test should be conducted by running the water for a couple of minutes or so to purge the lines of water that has been sitting in the pipes. The level of lead in water after the lines have been purged should not exceed 5 ug/l. If it does, corrective measures should be taken. Concentrations that are regularly below 5 ug/l in the purged water means that flushing of the lines should become a routine prior to use, and periodic re-testing would be appropriate to ensure that this approach remains effective.

INVESTIGATE AND MITIGATE

When excessive lead levels are detected, the next step is to identify the source. Water companies and water utilities test for lead (among many other chemicals) and are required by the EPA to reduce unacceptable levels. However, it is uncommon for municipal supplies to be contaminated with lead at the source.

Homes that have private water wells may have to sample their water directly at the well (before it goes through household piping) to establish the baseline quality of their water supply. In some rare instances, well pumps with brass components leach lead into the water. On the reasonable assumption that neither a public water supply nor a private well is contaminated with lead, the probable sources are the pipes connecting the home to a water main or the plumbing that distributes water throughout the house.

There is a variety of options available to reduce the levels of lead in your drinking water. Perhaps the most expensive, but also a permanently effective approach, would be to completely replace all plumbing in the house that includes lead pipe and/or lead solder. Resorting to bottled water is also an option, but it is both costly and inconvenient. As discussed, flushing the water to purge lines before drinking or cooking, is a simple and effective approach for some circumstances, provided that the "after purge" level is below 5 ug/l.

Distillation, filtration, and reverse-osmosis systems are efficient and effective to varying degrees. For example, calcite filters can reduce the acidity of water (raise the pH), and thereby reduce the corrosive effect on piping and solder. Chapter 9 discusses a number of drinking water contaminants and treatment measures in more detail.

REFERENCE

1993 Environmental Almanac, Compiled by World Resources Institute, Hammond, Allen, Ed. in Chief, Houghton Mifflin Co., New York, 1992, p. 28.

INDOOR AIR QUALITY

"Take a straw and throw it up into the air – you shall see by that which way the wind is."

John Selden

TAKE A DEEP BREATH

While issues of air pollution came to the public's attention in a big way twenty-five years ago, no one would have guessed that issues of interior air quality would eventually represent greater health concerns than the smoggy skies outside. Over the past ten to fifteen years it has become increasingly recognized that the quality of the indoor air we breathe is a primary source of environmental health risks.

The conventional wisdom has been that you are most safe at home; regrettably, it is often the exact opposite. Interior air quality has gotten worse and our exposure to pollutants has increased due to a number of conditions.

Energy efficient construction reduces ventilation; building materials give off contaminants; natural and manmade pollutants infiltrate from outside;

hazardous materials are used and stored in the home; combustion systems degrade the quality of the air in our homes.

In 1990, the United States Environmental Protection Agency (EPA) considered *indoor* air pollution *the* principal source of cancer risks to our health. EPA studies of comparative risks rank indoor air quality in the top five public health threats. Aside from the more widely recognized contaminants such as radon, lead-based paint dust, and asbestos (Chapters 4, 5, and 11, respectively), indoor air pollution comes from a surprising number of unsuspected sources. The adverse health effects from indoor contaminant sources range from physical discomfort to respiratory diseases and death.

CLOSE QUARTERS

Why is air in the home such a risk? As is the case with almost all contaminants, the potential health effects are directly related to the duration of exposure and concentrations of the pollutants. People spend the vast majority of their lives indoors - either working, or at home, sleeping, eating, etc. With respect to infants, the sick, and the elderly, the quality of interior air becomes especially important. These people have heightened sensitivities due to weak or developing systems and because they may spend up to 100% of their lives indoors. The result is a significant duration of exposure.

EPA studies show that as many as ten times more types of harmful contaminants (at up to one hundred times higher concentrations) can be found in interior air versus exterior air. The sources of the contaminants can be found throughout homes in addition to the migration of exterior contaminants into homes.

Harmful compounds will naturally accumulate to higher levels inside than outside. This accumulation is due to reduced air movement, which results in less dilution and dispersion of the contaminants. The problem has been compounded over the last twenty-five years by the need to build increasingly weatherproof and energy-efficient homes or the renovation of older homes to make them more efficient.

WHERE IS IT COMING FROM?

Indoor air pollutants originate from many sources, most of them are not commonly suspected of causing serious harm. Carpeting, paint, furniture, paneling, adhesives and cabinetry can all emit volatile organic compounds (VOCs), which can be irritants and in some cases cancer-causing. The incomplete combustion of fuels and improper venting of water heaters, fireplaces, and dryers can all create carbon monoxide, which, at sufficient levels, can kill.

Increasingly, molds and other biological contaminants have also been recognized as triggers for severe allergies and in some cases even more serious lung conditions. In addition, groundwater and soil contamination from underground storage tank leaks and other hazardous waste discharges can migrate over considerable distances and produce harmful air pollutants that seep into homes. Hazardous waste and contamination issues are discussed in further detail in Chapter 8.

Many indoor air contaminants can adversely affect your health at concentrations that are extremely low. In many cases, the levels that can damage your health are less than the concentration at which the contaminant can be smelled, or it may have no odor at all. The lack of an obvious odor can result in circumstances where there are adverse health symptoms without any readily obvious explanation.

Because the sources of indoor air contaminants can be so large, so too are the health effects. Many chemical compounds cause reactions that range from flu-like symptoms, to typical allergic traits such as congestion, shortness of breath, and eye and throat irritation. Exposures to higher concentrations of some contaminants, and for a longer duration, can cause more pronounced reactions such as dizziness, headaches, vision problems, rashes, blood in the lungs, and death.

CARBON MONOXIDE

Carbon monoxide accumulation in the home has recently become more widely recognized as a serious threat to your health. It is known as a silent killer because it is a tasteless, odorless, and colorless gas, which can poison and kill without you ever becoming aware of the threat. Consequently, carbon monoxide is the number one cause of accidental poisonings in the United States. An estimated 200 to 1,000 people die each year because of carbon monoxide poisoning in the home. It is likely that many thousands more become seriously sick without knowing the cause.

Carbon monoxide is one of many by-product gases that are produced during the incomplete combustion of fuels such as natural gas, oil, kerosene, wood, etc. The complete combustion of fuel produces carbon *dioxide*. Unfortunately, there are a large number of sources that can generate carbon monoxide in the home. Furnaces, kitchen ranges, pilot lights, clothes dryers, wood burning stoves, oil lamps, kerosene and gas heaters, fireplaces - all produce carbon monoxide. Unless the equipment is in good working order and flues and chimneys vent properly, there is a significant potential for the buildup of carbon monoxide in the home. Figure 6.1 illustrates some of the many potential sources.

HEALTH EFFECTS

When carbon monoxide is breathed into the lungs it reacts with hemoglobin and interferes with the oxygen carrying capacity of the blood. If the oxygen delivered to tissues and organs such as the heart, brain, and nervous system is reduced, the effect can be severe.

Early symptoms of carbon monoxide poisoning include drowsiness, dizziness, headaches, nausea and fatigue. Unfortunately, these symptoms often mimic colds or influenza, and many people may not recognize that they are being poisoned. The confusion may be heightened because colds and the flu are more prevalent during colder weather when the use of heating systems, stoves, fireplaces, etc. is increased. Consequently, carbon monoxide poisoning tends

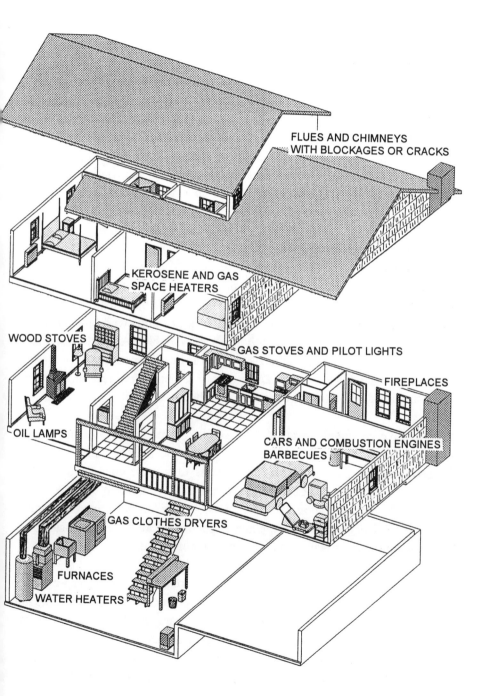

FIGURE 6.1 - POTENTIAL SOURCES OF CARBON MONOXIDE

to be more common during the heating season in colder climates when homes are shut tight for energy efficiency.

Continued exposure to high enough levels of carbon monoxide can cause vomiting, dizziness, unconsciousness and death within minutes to hours depending upon the concentrations and the susceptibility of the person. Because the poisoning often occurs during sleep, when there is little external ventilation (doors and windows not being opened), the victims are often completely unaware and simply never wake up.

DETECTION AND INVESTIGATION

Just as smoke detectors should be in all homes, so too should carbon monoxide monitors. A variety of plug-in and battery operated models are on the market and cost typically less than $75. Clock radios with built-in carbon monoxide detectors have also recently become available. At least one monitor should be located near sleeping areas, where the best chance exists for alerting occupants. The Consumer Product Safety Commission recommends one carbon monoxide monitor for each floor of a home.

It is a relatively straightforward task to assess a home for potential generators of carbon monoxide gas and the potential for the gas to accumulate inside. A licensed contractor can check heating systems for proper combustion. Older less-efficient furnaces are of more concern than more modern equipment that may include sealed combustion chambers, which produce more complete burning. Pilot lights and gas appliances should be inspected to ensure that they have blue flames, which indicate optimal combustion.

Chimneys and flues for fireplaces, stoves and furnaces should be inspected for blockages and/or cracks that could allow carbon monoxide to remain within or perhaps seep back into the home. Attached garages also are a source for carbon monoxide generated by idling automobiles or other combustion engines. Even with the garage door open, it is never a good practice to barbecue inside or to allow a car, lawnmower, or other engine to idle within a garage.

VOLATILE ORGANIC COMPOUNDS & FORMALDEHYDE

Volatile organic compounds (VOCs) represent a broad grouping of hundreds of chemical substances that, by definition, readily evaporate, and therefore, can produce harmful concentrations of chemicals in the surrounding air. Many volatile organics are emitted from common petroleum substances and similar products such as gasoline, turpentine and paint thinner. Additional volatile compounds come from cosmetics, waxes, cleaners, paints, finishing materials, construction adhesives, and solvents like dry cleaning fluids and degreasers. EPA studies have found that regardless of whether you live in a rural or urban area, concentrations of common organic contaminants were two to five times higher indoors than outdoors.

HEALTH EFFECTS

In most cases, the volatile organics that exist in a home are at low concentrations and/or occur for a short enough duration that the health effects are inconsequential. However, some volatile compounds are known or suspected carcinogens. At sufficient concentrations, other volatile compounds can also cause adverse impacts to your health. Exposure to and inhalation of some volatiles can result in eye and throat irritation, rashes, lung and mucous membrane irritation, dizziness, headaches, memory problems and nausea. An exposure to high concentrations or long-term exposures to variable levels can result in severe health problems, including damage to the central nervous system.

SOURCES

Potential sources for volatiles exist throughout the home. Many homeowners have a tendency to pour anything down any drain. In the case of home workshops, home "laboratories" or simple household maintenance products, this improper disposal represents many chemicals being poured into floor drains, sink drains, or sumps. This can create a long-term source of noxious vapors within nearby septic systems, in plumbing, and beneath floor slabs. The discharged materials can also find their way into private well supplies.

If possible, avoid storing volatile-containing products. Rather than storing or throwing away excess product, buy in smaller quantities. If storing chemicals and other petroleum products is necessary, use an exterior location instead of under sinks, in basements or in attached garages. This will reduce volatile concentrations in the home and will also isolate fire hazards.

Aside from the common and perhaps obviously "smelly" items discussed above, many materials used in construction and home finishing products can emit relatively unnoticed volatile vapors. Synthetic carpets, especially when new, may give off chemical vapors. Textiles, pre-pasted wallpaper, cabinetry and other wood products may emit a volatile compound vapor known as formaldehyde.

FORMALDEHYDE

Formaldehyde is a chemical used in the manufacture of many building products. It can also be produced in a home during the combustion of fuels. Formaldehyde may be recognized as embalming fluid with a very distinctive and pungent odor, but at typical concentrations in the home, the gas is usually odorless.

Exposure at sufficient levels can irritate the eyes, nose, throat, and lungs, and cause coughing and headaches. It can also trigger asthma attacks. Additionally, formaldehyde causes cancer in laboratory animals and is a suspected human carcinogen. Figure 6.2 illustrates some of the many volatile organic and formaldehyde sources in and around the home.

The release of volatiles such as formaldehyde from some home materials can occur over years until the emitted concentrations become negligible. Environmental conditions such as higher temperature and higher humidity can accelerate the release of formaldehyde.

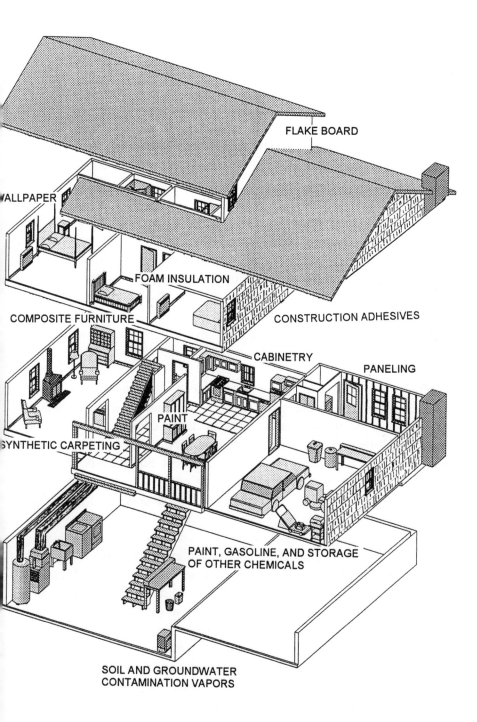

FIGURE 6.2 - POTENTIAL SOURCES OF VOLATILE ORGANICS

In most cases, older homes and the materials within have existed long enough that volatile contaminants, which may have been present, have had sufficient time to "off-gas". However, many homes for sale have recently undergone renovations. Fresh paint, wallpaper, carpeting, replacement cabinetry may all be relatively recent additions. Because these items are new, they will have had less time to vent and the VOC/formaldehyde levels that are sometimes released can be expected to be higher. Individuals with increased sensitivity need to be aware of the potential exposure.

The number of products that include formaldehyde is surprisingly widespread. Urea-formaldehyde glue is used in the manufacture of particleboard and fiberboard, which is made by compressing wood fragments into panels. Particleboard is common in inexpensive furniture (items with veneers, bookcases, closet organizers, juvenile furniture, entertainment units, etc). Formaldehyde resin is also often in kitchen and bath cabinets, doors, and in flake board which is a less expensive alternative to plywood in sub-floors and walls.

In recent years, mobile homes and pre-fabricated homes tended to have higher formaldehyde levels because of increased percentages of particleboard and other pressed wood products in their construction. The U.S. Department of Housing and Urban Development now restricts the formaldehyde levels that can be emitted in this type of construction. Although finished products do not carry a warning, particleboard bought in its unfinished form may include precautions about possible eye and respiratory irritation due to formaldehyde release.

In 1982, the Consumer Product Safety Commission banned the use of urea-formaldehyde foam insulation in homes and in schools. This action was taken after complaints of respiratory irritation developed following extensive use of the product to insulate home and building walls in the 1970s. The ban was overturned by a U.S. Court of Appeals; but the net effect has been a significant reduction in use of the insulation. Although homes built before 1982 have a stronger possibility of urea-formaldehyde insulation, it is likely that if significant concentrations of formaldehyde were present, it would have off-gassed and vented from the house over the intervening years.

MOLDS

Molds and mildew are terms for fungi that grow on most any surface if there is sufficient moisture. Aside from the obvious staining and other physical damage to walls, floors, and furniture that can be caused by excessive moisture, for many people the mold that results can be a much bigger problem. Molds, and associated airborne spores, frequently are unseen and unsuspected sources of serious respiratory problems.

HEALTH EFFECTS

Besides the staining and odor problems, airborne mold spores (alive or dead) can cause allergic reactions and much more severe responses in a surprisingly large number of people. Aside from the fact that the spores can be a source of physical irritation such as sneezing and watery eyes, molds can give off volatile organic vapors. Depending on the types of mold and an individual's reaction, the health effects can range from deep congestion, throat, eye, and nose irritation, to shortness of breath and lethargy. A type of mold known as "black mold" can cause bleeding lungs in some highly susceptible children.

SOURCES

Although molds can grow almost anywhere, warm, moist areas in a home are most conducive to growth. Problem areas of mold that are readily apparent, such as in humid/wet bathrooms, are typically easy to address and remedy. However, there are other locations throughout a home that can promote the development of undetected mold.

Areas often unseen or overlooked include leaking pipes within walls, wet areas in basements and behind cabinets, damp areas beneath floors, wet foundations with poor drainage around the exterior of a home, moisture in central heating and cooling systems, humidifiers, damp homes due to excessive shade, and leaky roofs. Typically, if areas are just sufficiently moist, it will be an environment that can sustain mold. Figure 6.3 details potential moisture problem areas and possible mold growth locations.

Investigate a home for indications of former or active water damage due to leaks or flooding (warping of wallboard and paneling, stains, lifted wood floors, odors). Although suspect areas may appear dry on the surface, telltale signs may indicate moisture is trapped within the walls or beneath flooring. Testing kits are available to determine the presence of mold, though, in most cases, the discoloration, odor and obvious growth will tell you it is there.

WHAT CAN YOU DO?

Investigations of poor air quality in a home and the correction of problems can vary as widely as the sources of the problems. The primary mitigation measures involve identifying and directly addressing the circumstances that are impacting air quality. With most volatile organic problems, identification of and removal of the sources is generally easy. Use a good dose of common sense and remove items such as paints, gasoline, thinners, cleaners, pesticides, etc. from the house and store them in a shed, storage bin, or other location that receives ample ventilation. If sources cannot easily be removed (such as cabinets or flooring), increasing the amount of external ventilation will, in most cases, drastically improve internal air quality.

SURVEY AND ASSESS

The World Health Organization has recommended that indoor levels of total volatile organic compounds not exceed a total of 0.05 parts per million. Instruments are available (generally used only by professionals) to take total volatile organic readings throughout a home. Air samples can also be collected for laboratory analyses to identify the specific types of volatile compounds that may be present. Further testing can be performed using reagent tubes where air is drawn through the tubes and reactions to specific types of contaminants will occur in the form of color changes. Ordinarily, the

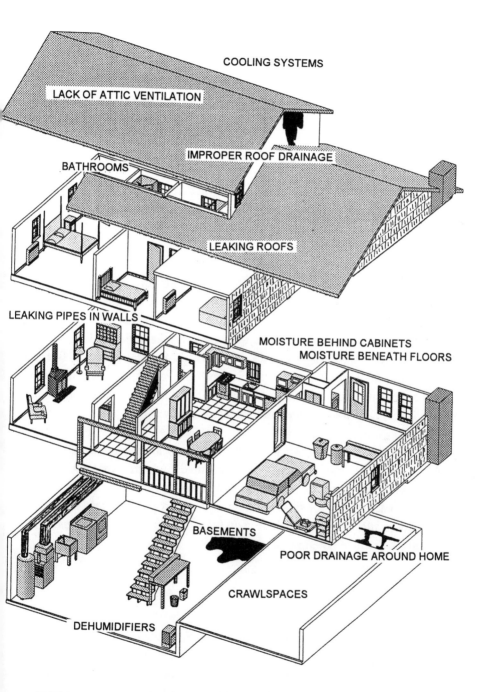

FIGURE 6.3 - SOURCES/LOCATIONS OF EXCESS MOISTURE

costs for a residential interior survey and laboratory analyses could range up to $2,000 - with costs heavily dependent upon the type and amount of samples that are collected for testing.

MITIGATION

The EPA believes that lower temperatures and lower humidity levels in the home will reduce the generation of volatile organic compounds. Therefore, air conditioning and dehumidifiers may be appropriate to keep a home cooler and the humidity levels below 50%.

If formaldehyde-emitting wood products already exist in a home, and removal outweighs the benefits or is cost prohibitive, sealing cabinets and other suspected wood products with finishes can block the release of formaldehyde vapors. The sealing should be done with a polyurethane or similar substance that has low or no volatile content. If practical, new cabinetry or furniture should be allowed to off-gas outside before installation. Storing items in a garage or screened porch for several months (if the time is available) will help reduce the formaldehyde concentrations significantly.

People who are highly sensitive to VOCs, such as formaldehyde, should ensure that their homes are built from formaldehyde-free materials. Solid wood cabinets and furniture, fiberglass insulation and traditional plywood will eliminate some of the potential formaldehyde sources. Carpets made from natural fibers such as wool, or bare wood floors with smaller area and throw rugs, can also reduce potential volatile vapors.

VENTILATION

Venting is the best option for situations where elimination is not feasible (such as could be the case with foam insulation or flake-board construction). One thing in your favor is that volatiles dissipate rapidly. Proper ventilation throughout a home is a simple and usually inexpensive cure for most indoor air-quality problems. Circulation of interior air with better exterior air can mitigate radon, volatile organic, and moisture problems. In colder climates, this may be practical for only a portion of each year due to the costs associated with heat loss. There are however, heat exchange devices that can be installed to retain the heat in the system when warmed interior air is replaced with cooler exterior air for venting purposes.

Provided that the air you vent with is relatively low in humidity and well circulated, mold and mildew problems can also be corrected. The growth should be stopped first and removed, which can be accomplished with commercial products, or where appropriate, a bleach or detergent solution. Applying these materials should also inhibit re-growth. Moisture problems can be further eased by using a dehumidifier with a target humidity level of less than 50%. It is important to regularly empty, clean and disinfect a dehumidifier; otherwise, they can be part of the problem by breeding molds and bacteria. Moisture can also be controlled by making sure wet areas such as kitchens and baths have exhaust fans, and basements and attics are well ventilated.

Airborne particulate problems such as mold spores, other allergens, and asbestos fibers can be removed with portable high efficiency particulate air (HEPA) filters. In some models, with charcoal and supplemental filtration, an added benefit is the removal of small amounts of odors as well as volatile organic compounds. To improve air throughout a home, filters and treatment systems can also be incorporated into the central heating and cooling systems of the house. These devices can humidify air when needed, dehumidify when needed, and provide differing levels of filtration.

7

OUTDOOR AIR QUALITY

"As soon as I had gotten out of the heavy air of Rome and from the
stink of the smoky chimneys thereof, which, being stirred, poured fourth
whatever pestilential vapors and soot they had enclosed in them, I felt
an alteration of my disposition."

Seneca, AD 61

NEED SOME BREATHING ROOM?

Air pollution, apparently nothing new. Nevertheless, Seneca did not
know how good he had it. He was fortunate in the fact that he and
the people of Ancient Rome did not have to breathe automobile
exhaust, incinerator emissions, ground-level ozone, fallout, and the airborne
by-products of modern chemical processes.

In the United States today, we find that the quality of outdoor air varies
considerably from place to place. These variations are a function of the types
of development, weather and seasonal changes, and even topographic
landforms. Evaluating the air quality in a community means that we need to
assess the types of pollutants emitted, the potential for airborne contaminants

to amass to unhealthy levels, and how near our homes are to potential contaminant sources.

Air pollution, like all types of pollution, is the accumulation of potentially hazardous compounds that can significantly affect your quality of life as well as your health. We breathe pollutants from a tremendous number of sources. Motor vehicles, chemical process emissions, utility smokestacks, major fires and fuel combustion - all discharge many tons of pollutants into the air every day.

Exterior air pollutants come in six major forms: airborne particulates, carbon monoxide, hydrocarbons, sulfur dioxide, nitrogen oxides, and photochemical oxidants. These contaminants, however, do not only exist in their primary form, but can also combine with other contaminants and/or be altered by environmental parameters to produce secondary contaminants such as smog and acid rain.

WHERE DOES IT COME FROM?

The majority of people will drive by a factory or refinery smokestack and consider it and others like it as the major source of pollutants in our air. In reality, however, the automobile they are driving (and others like it) is the true source of the largest percentage of air pollution in the United States.

The combustion of fossil fuels such as petroleum, gas, wood, coal, etc. produces carbon dioxide and water. Combustion, however, also produces by-products of carbon monoxide, ash, metals, additional hydrocarbons, acids, sulfur and nitrogen oxides and many other contaminants. The use of fossil fuels in heating systems, fireplaces, barbecue grills, refuse burning and electricity generation all release massive quantities of pollutants.

In addition to the contaminants from combustion processes, industrial and manufacturing facilities release vast quantities of toxic chemicals and other particulate matter. These pollutants vary as widely as the chemicals that are used and the materials produced in the manufacturing processes. When pollutants are released, they may be in the form of dusts, vapors, aerosols, fumes and gases. Steel and other metals manufacturing, petroleum refineries, power generating facilities, sewage treatment plants, and waste incinerators are also major sources of noxious odors, oxides, toxic chemicals, and airborne particulates.

CARBON MONOXIDE

Carbon monoxide is a major and potentially lethal indoor air contaminant (Chapter 6). The primary source for carbon monoxide outdoors is vehicular exhaust. Exposure to high concentrations (typically in metropolitan areas, but increasingly in the traffic-jammed suburbs) can reduce the ability of the body to carry oxygen in the blood. Carbon monoxide breathed into the lungs reacts with hemoglobin and reduces the oxygen that is delivered to tissues and organs.

SMOG AND OZONE

Smog is most commonly recognized as the hazy "air that we can see" - typically on a hot summer afternoon. Smog is created by a variety of volatile organic chemicals, petroleum vapors, and combustion by-products released into the air. Sunlight and heat then act like a natural chemistry lab to accelerate chemical reactions, involving the volatile compounds and nitrogen oxides, to produce dozens of noxious compounds, including ground-level ozone.

Although ozone is a beneficial protective layer in the upper atmosphere, which blocks harmful solar radiation, ozone at ground-level causes respiratory irritation, aggravates asthma, decreases lung capacity, and can even inhibit plant growth and decrease agricultural yields. Mortality rates amongst the young and old increase during heavy smog events. In the summer months, the adverse effects of smog are enhanced and death rates climb due to warm temperatures and an increase in outdoor exercise and other activities. In December of 1952, an extremely lethal smog in London, England killed an estimated 4,000 people.

PARTICULATES, SULFUR DIOXIDES

Particulate matter covers a wide range of solid and liquid pollutants in an aerosol form. Industrial discharges, large-scale forest fires, incinerators and open-burning dumps all produce airborne particulate matter (ash, soot, dust and fibers) as well as toxics that irritate the lungs and eyes.

Smelting operations, paper manufacturing, and oil and coal combustion also emit sulfur dioxide and nitrogen oxides. Both of these gases can cause respiratory problems and, when combined with moisture in the atmosphere, acid rain can result. Because of the corrosive nature of acid rain (lower pH), house and automobile paint can be damaged as well as vegetation and lakes and streams. Due to the prevalent use of coal and other heavy industries, acid rain has long been an issue in the Midwest. Prevailing weather patterns carry the acid rain problem to the Northeast and Canada.

LEAD

Though not as prevalent as it was ten to twenty years ago, airborne lead can be a serious air contaminant. Combustion of leaded gasoline, manufacturing processes, smelting, lead-contaminated dust, waste-oil combustion and trash incineration, can all release lead into the atmosphere.

Lead that is inhaled can be absorbed directly into the bloodstream, where it accumulates in the blood, bones and organs. High levels of lead in blood cause nerve damage, birth defects and learning disabilities. Chapter 5 discusses household lead (lead-based paint and lead in drinking water) in greater detail.

THE HEALTH RISK

Of course, the respiratory system represents the primary route of exposure to air pollution. Consequently, the olfactory system and the lungs are most commonly affected. However, it is not unusual to experience circulation problems as well as skin and eye irritation when exposed to certain types of air pollution. As with most environmental contaminants, the young, the elderly, and people with previously existing conditions such as asthma, heart disease and emphysema are most susceptible to the effects of air pollution.

In extreme cases, especially when pre-existing health problems are involved, exposures to significant levels of air pollution can result in respiratory arrest and even death. The health problems that may develop after inhalation or exposure to air pollutants may be immediate (and minor), such as simple irritation of the lungs or eyes. Alternatively, the effects may be delayed for years. For instance, the development of lung cancer may not occur until after years of long-term exposure.

Air pollution may not always come from readily apparent sources or have a verifiable or obvious toxic effect. Excessive use of fertilizers, pesticides and herbicides by golf courses, homeowners, and agricultural operations may not appear as an obvious source of problems, but can result in airborne contaminants that cause extreme reactions in some people. In the instance of industrial and agricultural operations, or municipal sewage, the odors can be the source of nausea, vomiting and headaches. Though these symptoms may be short lived, the adverse influence on the quality of life can be significant.

CARE TO STEP OUTSIDE FOR A BREATH OF FRESH AIR?

Fortunately, exterior air quality has improved dramatically over the past twenty-five years. The Federal Clean Air Act, and better technology for controlling emissions, have cut the levels of most major pollutants steadily since the early 1970s. However, according to the EPA, in 1996, approximately 46 million people throughout the United States lived in counties where at least one of the acceptable air quality standards were regularly exceeded. Figures 7.1, 7.2, and 7.3 illustrate the general locations of counties across the United States where common air quality standards have been persistently exceeded.

Homes in heavily populated or industrialized valleys tend to have higher concentrations of air pollutants.   Due to the geographic isolation by surrounding hills and mountains, air movement is reduced and pollution is not readily dissipated.   In the Los Angeles Basin, air quality standards are regularly exceeded throughout the year due to stagnant air masses. Areas of the country with relatively immobile weather patterns also typically have more air pollution problems.

LOCATION, LOCATION, LOCATION

Overall, the choices are few for those of us who want to avoid locations with high levels of air pollution. Because the sources can rarely be eliminated, avoiding the sources is the next best option. If you can, try to live in areas with reduced traffic or at least live in areas with less traffic congestion.

If living in or near an urban or industrial area cannot be avoided, consider the prevailing wind patterns and try to live upwind of known sources.   Often pollutants such as ozone are higher downwind from a city than within a city itself. What must also be remembered, is that air pollution occurs not only on the local level, but on the regional level as well. Pollutants from large cities can travel hundreds of miles with the fallout and airborne contaminants adversely affecting downwind populations in rural areas.

Over the past several years, many cities and some states have mandated the use of cleaner burning fuels to reduce vehicular emissions, especially during the winter. There has been some controversy, however, over whether fuel additives to reduce the emissions are actually causing adverse health effects when petroleum that leaks from tanks find its way into water supplies.

Releases to the air from industry and utility generators vary widely from state to state. The amount of pollutants released is directly related to the type of

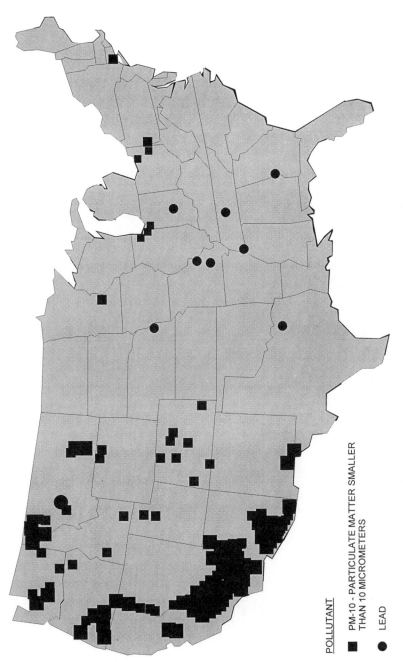

POLLUTANT

■ PM-10 - PARTICULATE MATTER SMALLER
THAN 10 MICROMETERS

● LEAD

(SOURCE: ADAPTED FROM USEPA AEROMETRIC INFORMATION RETRIEVAL SYSTEM, MARCH 1999.)

FIGURE 7.1 - APPROXIMATE COUNTY LOCATIONS WHERE AIR POLLUTION STANDARDS ARE PERSISTENTLY EXCEEDED

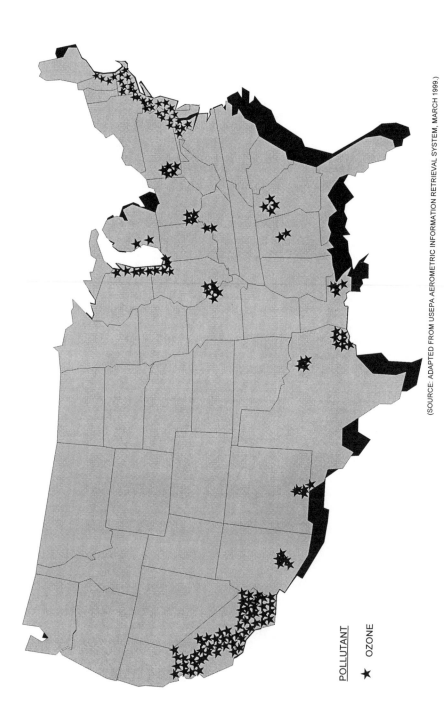

(SOURCE: ADAPTED FROM USEPA AEROMETRIC INFORMATION RETRIEVAL SYSTEM, MARCH 1999.)

FIGURE 7.2 - APPROXIMATE COUNTY LOCATIONS WHERE AIR POLLUTION STANDARDS ARE PERSISTENTLY EXCEEDED

POLLUTANT

★ OZONE

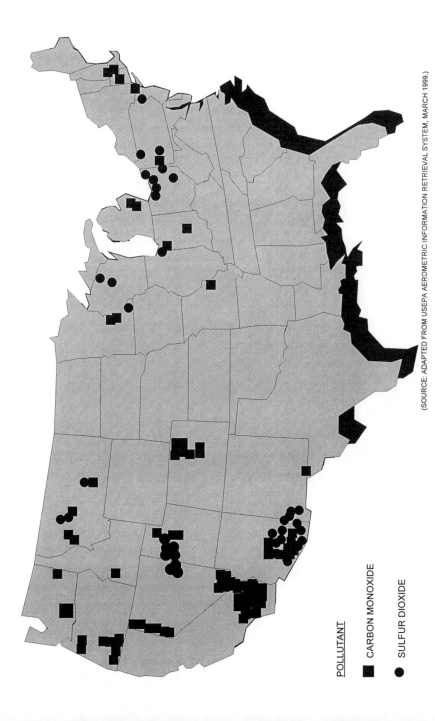

(SOURCE: ADAPTED FROM USEPA AEROMETRIC INFORMATION RETRIEVAL SYSTEM, MARCH 1999.)

FIGURE 7.3 - APPROXIMATE COUNTY LOCATIONS WHERE AIR POLLUTION STANDARDS ARE PERSISTENTLY EXCEEDED

POLLUTANT

■ CARBON MONOXIDE

● SULFUR DIOXIDE

industry and if they follow the law. For years it has been commonplace for
industry that cannot or is not willing to comply with regulations, to buy
pollution credits from other industries that can comply. The following tables
summarize data collected by the EPA with respect to toxic air emissions by
states and overall indications of air quality.

Table 7.1- Top Ten States for Air Emissions of Toxics, 1990.

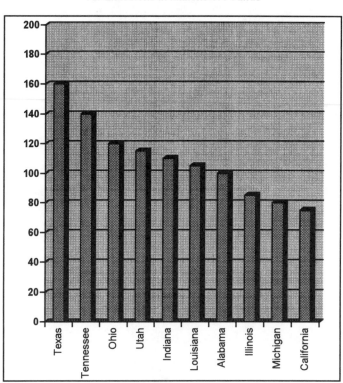

Air Emissions in Millions of Pounds

Source: Adapted from Environmental Almanac, 1993, p.88. Data from USEPA, 1990 Toxics
Release Inventory, Public Data Release (U.S.G.P.O., Washington, D.C., May 1992) Table 4,
p.23.

Table 7.2 - Average Air Quality (Pollutant Standards Index (PSI)) Based upon Daily Readings of Sulfur Dioxide, Nitrogen Oxides, Particulate Matter, Carbon Monoxide, and Ozone.

Metro Area	Avg. PSI	Metro Area	Avg. PSI
Honolulu	15	Tulsa	42
San Francisco-Oakland	20	Detroit	43
Kansas City	28	Grand Rapids	43
Washington, D.C.	32	Dallas - Ft. Worth	43
Pittsburgh	32	Milwaukee	44
Scranton	33	Las Vegas	44
Chicago	33	St. Louis	45
Louisville	33	Toledo	45
Albany	33	New York	46
Rochester	34	Columbus	46
Allentown	34	Jacksonville	46
Cleveland	35	Tampa-St. Petersburg	46
Harrisburg	35	Atlanta	47
Providence	35	Baton Rouge	47
Salt Lake City	36	El Paso	48
New Haven	36	Phoenix	48
Nashville	37	Memphis	49
Omaha	37	Tucson	49
Austin	38	Indianapolis	49
New Orleans	38	Bakersfield	51
Denver	39	Sacramento	51
Baltimore	39	Knoxville	52
Philadelphia	39	Charlotte	54
Worcester	39	San Diego	54
San Antonio	39	Houston	56
Cincinnati	40	Raleigh-Durham	56
Oklahoma City	41	Fresno	56
Dayton	42	Los Angeles	73
Orlando	42		

Source: Adapted from Environmental Almanac, 1993, p.201. Data from USEPA, Aerometric Information Retrieval System, Pollutant Standard Index Summary, 1990.

Table 7.3 - Unhealthy Air Pollution Days, 1990

Metro Area	Number of Unhealthy Days
Los Angeles	70
Houston	36
San Diego	14
New York	13
Baton Rouge	10
Fresno	10
Phoenix	8
Sacramento	6
Dallas - Fort Worth	5
El Paso	4
Philadelphia	4
Atlanta	3
Seattle - Tacoma	2
Grand Rapids	2
Tulsa	2
Baltimore	2

Source: Adapted from Environmental Almanac, 1993, p.203. Data from USEPA, Aerometric Information Retrieval System, Pollutant Standard Index Summary, 1990.

A CORNUCOPIA OF CONTAMINATION

"The great question of the seventies is: Shall we surrender to our
surroundings or shall we make our peace with nature and make reparations
for the damage we have done to our air, to our land, and to our water?"

Richard M. Nixon

"The supreme reality of our time is...
the vulnerability of this planet."

John F. Kennedy

HAZARDOUS HAZARDS - HOW BIG IS THE PROBLEM?

Over 300 million tons of hazardous waste are produced and disposed
of annually in the United States. Every year hundreds of new
chemicals are developed and incorporated with existing chemicals
into manufacturing processes, research activities, and consumer products.
Consequently, year after year thousands of properties throughout the United
States are discovered to be contaminated by intentional and unintentional
discharges of hazardous chemicals and wastes.

Because hazardous materials are ubiquitous in our communities and can readily migrate, virtually every residential property is subject to at least some risk for being contaminated. In order to assess the potential risk of living near and being exposed to hazardous substances, a homeowner must consider former as well as current hazardous material use and disposal practices in their community.

Accompanying modern manufacturing are the leaks, disposal activities, and routine emissions of hazardous materials to the air, soil and groundwater that cause widespread and persistent sources of contamination. The transportation of hazardous materials by truck, rail, and boat results in hundreds of accidental spills each year, many of which end up in requiring the evacuation of residents along transportation routes. Contained and sometimes not so contained wastes in 55-gallon drums, can commonly be found behind all manner of industrial sites, former farms and other facilities, and are often illegally dumped beside roadways or in a convenient patch of woods.

As contaminants are released to migrate through the environment, they can seriously affect the health of people who are exposed either directly or through secondary routes such as the food chain and tainted drinking water. Naturally, those most at risk live relatively close to and are downwind or geologically "downhill" from the properties or accident locations where the hazardous substances are released.

In addition to the health risks, there can be serious financial impacts to a homeowner. There are cases when the value of contaminated property may drop to less than zero, or a lender may refuse financing due to the contamination liability. Therefore, a potential problem can exist for virtually every home.

Hazardous chemicals and wastes are stored, used and disposed of in many ways and can readily be found in just about every part of every community. Aside from typical industrial and manufacturing locations, hazardous substances can be found at dry cleaners, printing facilities, vacant lots, farms, transportation facilities, service stations, repair shops, jewelers, landscapers, in underground tanks, in landfills, etc. At home we use and produce additional chemicals and waste in the form of cleaners, pesticides, petroleum, paints, automotive fluids, batteries, etc. With increased human exposures to raw chemicals and wastes, rates of disorders, disease and death have also climbed.

REGULATING THE PROBLEM

Most often, hazardous materials are properly handled. Nevertheless, cases of intentional and unintentional releases to the environment are regularly found in the headlines. Moreover, for every occurrence that makes the headlines, hundreds of others remain to be discovered. Often, discoveries come too late – only after the human and environmental damage has occurred.

In an attempt to address the management of wastes and degradation of the environment, more strict environmental regulations were passed during the 1970s and into the 1980s. However, an unintended consequence of the regulations was an increase in illegal dumping in many localities. Unscrupulous operators, trying to avoid the costs of proper handling and disposal of wastes, turned vacant lots, wooded areas, and abandoned mines into toxic dumps overnight. Because the wastes were deposited illegally, no one could know for sure what types of pollutants went in and what types of hazards would eventually come out.

WHAT IS SWEPT UNDER THE CARPET?

Hazardous wastes are generally chemical and petroleum wastes that can be in solid or liquid form and that exhibit potentially harmful characteristics. The wastes contain percentages of chemicals, which if the wastes were placed in a landfill, could be expected to leach hazardous chemicals after mixing with fluids that are generated in a landfill. Hazardous wastes have characteristics such as being corrosive, caustic, or radioactive, or other properties that include being readily ignitable or explosive.

Fortunately, most of the chemicals and wastes in our society are stored, used, and disposed of in a relatively safe manner. The vast majority of wastes that are generated today are sent to well built and managed, sanitary landfills and other transfer, storage and disposal facilities. However, for years this was not the case and wastes were regularly pumped, piped and dumped into any conveniently available drainage ditch, stream, former quarry or town dump. In most cases, dumping and discharge areas were little more than a hole in the ground with no regard to the long-term effects of the wastes on groundwater, streams and lakes.

LOVE CANAL

A drastic, but sadly not too unusual, example of careless disposal is what happened at the Love Canal in Niagara Falls, New York. The Hooker Chemical and Plastics Corporation had given a piece of property to the city in 1953. A school and housing development were subsequently built on the land. The fly in the ointment was that the area included an old canal that had been covered over, and into which the Hooker Corporation had dumped waste for twenty years before the dubious gift of the land to the city. Not until the early 1970s, long after the development of the land, was this toxic timebomb discovered – only after it had gone off.

Soil, both at the surface and in the subsurface, and groundwater had become contaminated with dozens of toxic materials and cancer-causing chemicals that had been disposed in the canal. Rates of miscarriages, birth defects, liver cancer, and other disorders were extremely high in the community. Ultimately, the entire area was classified as an official disaster and millions of dollars were spent on litigation, relocating families, and finally the cleanup of soil and groundwater.

BROWNFIELDS AND SUPERFUNDS

For decades, industrial operations in our country have routinely leaked and spilled hazardous substances in the normal course of doing business. Industry in some regions has decreased over the years, while surviving industry has moved out of the cities. Often they leave behind contaminated properties that are deemed too expensive for the diminished industry to rectify.

Attempts to clean up and reclaim these "brownfields" are being made, but with generally more lenient remediation standards, which result in less than completely clean properties. A compromise has been reached. In the interests of revitalizing industrial areas and the tax base of states and towns, higher levels of residual contamination have become acceptable.

The United States Environmental Protection Agency (EPA) and individual states regulate the usage and disposal of hazardous chemicals, materials, and wastes. The EPA designates the top priority contaminated properties as "Superfund Sites". They are found throughout the country. Cleanup of these sites over the past twenty years has been painstakingly slow. Most of the money is typically spent on legal wrangling, rather than the actual restoration of the environment to acceptable standards.

In addition to the Superfund sites, the EPA has listings of about 30,000 other properties that may contain hazardous materials or other forms of contamination. Illegal, inadvertent, and undiscovered contaminant releases and dumping probably account for tens of thousands of additional problem properties.

HEALTH EFFECTS

The effects of chemical substances on our health are almost as wide-ranging as the types of chemicals and waste that is generated. Since the onset of the industrial revolution in the late nineteenth century, our environment and often our health have become progressively, and in some instances irrevocably, degraded by the release of hazardous materials and wastes.

The hundreds of new chemicals that are brought to market each year must undergo toxicity testing via animal and other studies. Unfortunately, the testing is often biased, flawed, or human exposure is neither anticipated nor can it be reasonably extrapolated to humans. Therefore, the true effect of a chemical substance on a human being may not be accurately determined before use, storage or release into the environment. The incidents of misuse and intentional and unintentional releases of toxic materials can result in routes of exposure that are more hazardous than those that were ever expected (such as in the case of drinking water contamination).

Exposure to toxic chemicals and wastes comes in many forms. Accidental or intentional releases can result in direct contact. Contaminated soil, surface water and groundwater can all be additional mediums for exposure through ingestion or inhalation. Toxic chemicals can also be absorbed into the body by inhaling contaminated air and through the food chain by eating animals, fish, vegetables, etc. that have absorbed contaminants. As a result of smoke and fumes, hazardous substance exposures can also occur during fires and explosions.

TOUGH LESSONS

Despite toxicology studies of chemicals, the adverse impacts to humans are often not recognized until it is too late. Proper handling and disposal practices of chemicals and wastes have improved, but only after we discovered the harm caused by the old practices. Dozens of chemicals have been banned or severely regulated over the years, but not until we learned what they did to our bodies and our environment.

As new routes of exposure are identified and/or as disease rates rise, "acceptable" contamination criteria have been lowered or for some substances developed for the first time. Cancer clusters, birth defects, and other abnormal health impacts have increasingly been traced back to chemicals and handling practices that were thought safe or hadn't even been considered as potentially harmful in the first place. The following sections discuss several of the most common or notorious contaminants.

PCBs

Polychlorinated biphenyls (PCBs) were widely used in fluids in electrical transformers and many other devices for over sixty years. However, over just the past twenty years or so, PCBs have been shown to be carcinogenic and were linked to breast cancer. Unfortunately, due to indiscriminant dumping and spills, PCBs are widespread in the environment, and are also extremely enduring. PCBs bio-accumulate in food chains - with humans at the top of the chains. Effluent discharges by the General Electric Corporation are responsible for widespread PCB contamination of Hudson River sediments above New York City.

PETROLEUM

Products and waste that contain petroleum are everywhere in our society. Many components of gasoline, such as benzene and other additives, have been identified as carcinogenic and can cause a variety of additional disorders. Petroleum refining operations vent vast quantities of hazardous materials to the air. Oil, gasoline, and fuel discharges to the air, soil, and water occur regularly through underground and aboveground leaks and intentional and accidental discharges.

Millions of underground tanks store heating oils and motor fuels. Leaks are commonplace (Chapter 10 has an expanded discussion on underground storage tanks). Even small petroleum discharges can make vast quantities of groundwater unfit for drinking. Larger discharges can migrate significant distances through the subsurface, and can contaminate entire regional water supplies. Under the right conditions, petroleum releases can migrate into structures and produce harmful and even explosive vapors within a building.

DDT

Dichlorodiphenyltrichloroethane (DDT) was broadly used as an insecticide for more than thirty years until people recognized that the poison could bio-accumulate throughout food chains. Although DDT is largely responsible for drastic reductions in bald eagle populations, the full extent of its impact to the environment and humans has never been completely documented.

MERCURY

In the United States, thousands of tons of mercury are mined each year with much of it lost back into the environment. The harm caused by mercury discharges into a Japanese bay was not recognized until sharp increases in human birth defects were identified. People in the region had been eating fish, which had ingested mercury waste from industrial discharges.

Outside New York City, a group of people was renovating a former manufacturing building into residential condominiums and artist studios. After much of the work had been completed, and some of the residents had moved in, they discovered parts of the building were impregnated with mercury. Subsequent blood testing revealed mercury poisoning of some of the residents.

DIOXINS

Dioxins are a group of chemical compounds that are suspected of being highly toxic. Although extremely lethal to animals, dioxins have not been proven lethal to humans. However, as a component in Agent Orange (a Vietnam War era defoliant) a dioxin is believed to be responsible for a large number of birth defects and disorders amongst Vietnamese people and United States servicemen and their families.

In addition to defoliants, dioxins show up in wood preservatives, industrial effluents and oils. Dioxins also have been found in the discharges from paper mills and incinerator stacks. In one notorious case, the entire town of Times Beach, Missouri was permanently abandoned in 1983. The reason – oil contaminated with dioxin had been sprayed on roadways to keep dust levels down.

VARIOUS METALS

Discarded batteries and plating operations can be sources of lead, cadmium, zinc, chromium and other toxic metals that do not degrade over time and that will persist in the environment. The ingestion of toxic metals through contaminated food, dust, or water can represent a significant source of poisoning. Manufacturing operations, incinerators, coal burning, and legal and illegal disposal activities – all can release toxic metals into the air, which can ultimately settle as contaminated dust.

Soil that is contaminated with metals is sometimes used as fill material to develop properties. This soil is often imported from former industrial sites and other developed areas. By simply playing in yards developed with tainted fill or in areas that were manufacturing or disposal sites, children risk significant exposures to toxic metals.

VOCs

Volatile organic compounds (VOCs) represent a broad classification for a variety of toxic chemicals in widespread use. Many of these compounds are highly carcinogenic and a very little goes a very long way toward rendering entire public water systems and private wells unfit for use. Inhaling various volatile compounds can easily cause dizziness, headaches and nausea. In sufficient concentrations of the right compound, they can also kill.

Volatile compounds are often the primary component in solvents used by dry cleaning facilities, textile manufacturers, printers, machining, electronics and many other industries. Proper disposal of the waste material is expensive, so it was, and unfortunately still is, common for industry and other volatile chemical users to improperly store and discharge spent process materials that contain high levels of contaminants.

MISCELLANEOUS POLLUTANTS

Sewage effluent, pesticides, herbicides, and other contaminant discharges are often responsible for polluting surface water and groundwater supplies. These same contaminants pollute major waterways such as, the Long Island Sound in New York, Galveston Bay in Texas, the Chesapeake Bay in Maryland, and the Housatonic River in Massachusetts. This contamination poisons fish and shellfish, which are ultimately consumed by larger animals, including humans. Commercial fishing restrictions become commonplace and bottom sediments in water bodies will remain hazardous for years to come.

MIGRATION THROUGH THE ENVIRONMENT

Hazardous substances are vented to the air; spilled, stored and dumped on the ground surface; discharged into surface water bodies; buried beneath the ground; leaked into subsurface soils and groundwater; stored in exposed containment systems; and pumped into groundwater via subsurface injection wells. The result is a vast array of migration routes and hazards for humans and the environment as a whole.

A release of hazardous materials to the environment transfers contaminants into the medium (air, soil, and/or water) where the discharge occurs. The resulting pollutant concentrations will largely depend on the original levels, the physical characteristics of the contaminant, the media characteristics, and the environmental conditions. Leaks from underground tanks, piping, drywells, or spills directly to the ground naturally result in contamination of the surrounding soil. A one-time release, in sufficient quantity, or a steady release over time will migrate through the soil (enhanced by gravity and precipitation). Often, the migrating contaminants will ultimately encounter surface water and/or groundwater, and thus sources of drinking water.

Contamination in groundwater will generally move due to gravity. However, under certain conditions, pumping water from supply wells alters flow and can accelerate the spread of contaminants in groundwater. Because virtually all drinking water in the United States comes from either surface water (lakes, ponds, streams, reservoirs) or groundwater, everyone is at risk of exposure regardless of their proximity to the original source of contamination. Figure 8.1 illustrates some of the sources of hazardous materials in our environment as well as potential migration and exposure routes.

Most everyone is aware of some notorious chemicals, and now it seems commonsense that proper use and disposal practices must be maintained. But what is the next DDT or PCB that we may be living with? While contamination sources and the health impacts become apparent in many cases, we have little knowledge about the long-term effects of the unseen and low level pollutants that are continuously migrating through the environment.

HISTORICAL SOURCES

Because many environmental contaminants persist in nature, you must not only be concerned about discharges from active operations, but historical discharges as well. As was the case with the Love Canal, many residential areas throughout the country have been built on former industrial zones or on dumping grounds for manufacturing operations and other wastes. Many homes also have been constructed on fill materials, such as industrial waste and demolition debris, that were imported from contaminated sources for the purpose of leveling building sites.

In northern New Jersey communities in the 1980s and 1990s, (see Chapter 4), hundreds of properties were found to have excessively high levels of radon. The radon, however, was not due to naturally occurring uranium, but rather due to contaminated soils that had been dumped as industrial waste and later reused as fill. A nightmare followed for dozens of families.

Many residential communities are developed on former farms and other agricultural areas. Though prior agricultural use of the property may seem innocuous (because of the absence of industrial operations); the potential for waste disposal and contaminants such as pesticides and herbicides must still be considered.

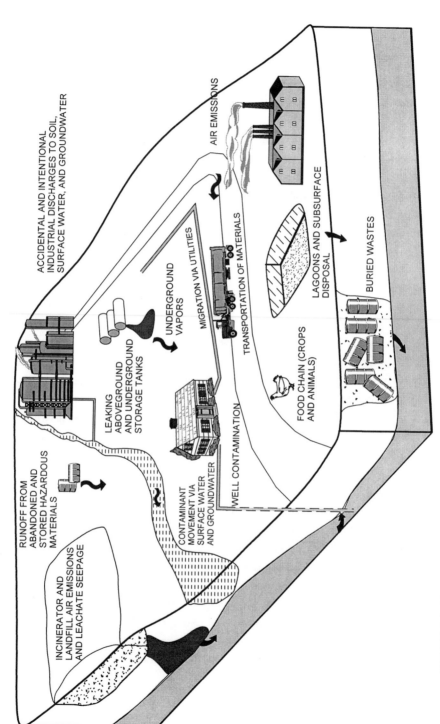

FIGURE 8.1 - HAZARDOUS MATERIAL SOURCES AND POTENTIAL MIGRATION/EXPOSURE ROUTES

Property thought to have been previously undeveloped is not always what it seems. Several years ago, I became involved in a residential construction project that encountered rather unexpected conditions. On the surface, it appeared to be a new residential community on formerly undeveloped woodland. However, after several million-dollar homes were built, a new lot revealed that the area had in fact been previously developed; the excavation for a house foundation encountered petroleum floating on the water table. Further exploration revealed an underground tank and other waste had been dumped exactly where the new home was to be placed. Subsequent investigations of the site history revealed that the property had been a fish hatchery. When it became obsolete, it served as a convenient and illegal dumping ground.

The circumstances ultimately became public knowledge and regulatory authorities became involved. The question persists, however, as to how many problems are never identified or acknowledged at similar sites across the United States. Chapter 12 discusses how to investigate the environmental history and condition of a property.

DRIVE THROUGH CONTAMINATION

The handling and disposal of hazardous materials is big business, and so is the transportation and interstate trade of the waste. Rails, roads, and waterways regularly move hazardous materials, and, of course, accidents and spills happen. A homeowner needs to consider how close a home is to major transportation thoroughfares as a potential risk.

Even relatively normal vehicular traffic can be an environmental hazard. Tractor trailers and large trucks are routinely involved in accidents; the rupture of large diesel tanks may spill as much as a two hundred gallons of fuel. In one case several years ago, I was involved in a project where a tractor-trailer veered off a road and crashed into a home. Unfortunately for the homeowner, in a terrible set of coincidences, the tanks on the truck ruptured and spilled diesel fuel directly into an eighteenth-century stone well.

RADIATION

Just as sources of chemical pollutants represent significant health concerns, so do operations that include radioactive materials and associated waste sites. The physiological effects of radiation are well documented. Radioactive-decay emissions can cause cancer, genetic damage and death. Radioactive releases from the Brookhaven National Laboratory on Long Island, New York are suspected by many as a contributing factor (along with pesticides) to the highest breast cancer rate in the nation.

When everything goes right, the use of radioactive materials and the corresponding disposal of waste can be accomplished safely. Unfortunately, *everything* hardly ever goes right. In 1979, the Three Mile Island nuclear power plant near Harrisburg, Pennsylvania partially melted down. As one of two reactors lost its coolant, the reactor overheated, which eventually released radiation into the air and into the adjacent Susquehanna River. Local communities were evacuated and, because of newly heightened public concerns, the nuclear industry has never fully recovered.

TOO FAST FOR OUR OWN GOOD

Ever since the development of the first atomic bomb and the harnessing of nuclear energy for power, we have had to deal with radioactive waste streams (that are not so easy to deal with). Types of radioactive waste range from low-level to high-level with several degrees of hazard in-between. These wastes are generated as byproducts in nuclear power generation, industrial processes and weapons programs. The more than fifty years worth of nuclear research and weapons buildup during the Cold War, created sites throughout the United States with severe radioactive contaminant problems.

The volume of radioactive waste generated during the Cold War far out-paced our ability, and perhaps our desire, to properly handle the waste products. Throughout the arms race, the United States government largely exempted itself from environmental regulations on emissions, waste handling, treatment, and disposal.   The result is numerous facilities with vast areas of soil, groundwater, surface water and surrounding air that are seriously contaminated.   However, for decades the military generally prevented the public from knowing much about the magnitude of the problems.   Figure 8.2 indicates a number of contaminated radioactive sites across the United States.

At the majority of radioactively contaminated sites, wastes stored in leaking tanks and lagoons have migrated into groundwater.   As precipitation hits radioactive soils, the surface runoff becomes contaminated and can ultimately end up in lakes and streams.   Contaminated soils also remain as a long-term source for groundwater pollution.   Releases from nuclear facilities over the years have caused pollution that represents billions of dollars in cleanup costs. Most of these sites are now being cleaned up under federal programs.

The potential for adverse health effects to residents near radioactive sites is significant.   Only over the past ten years or so has information about the level of contamination at some of these most severely contaminated sites become available.   Not until 1990 did the U.S. Department of Energy acknowledge that radioactive airborne releases, from the Hanford Reservation in Hanford, Washington, created serious health risks to area residents.

SEEK AND YE SHALL FIND

Hazardous materials exist in every area of our communities. Wastes and raw chemicals can be found in all of these areas.

➢   At the point of manufacture.
➢   At the point of use.
➢   Where waste products are generated.
➢   Where wastes are stored
➢   At illegal dump and discharge sites.
➢   Leaking into and moving through the environment; i.e. through the air, soil, and water.
➢   At treatment and disposal facilities.
➢   In transit via rail, road, or boat.

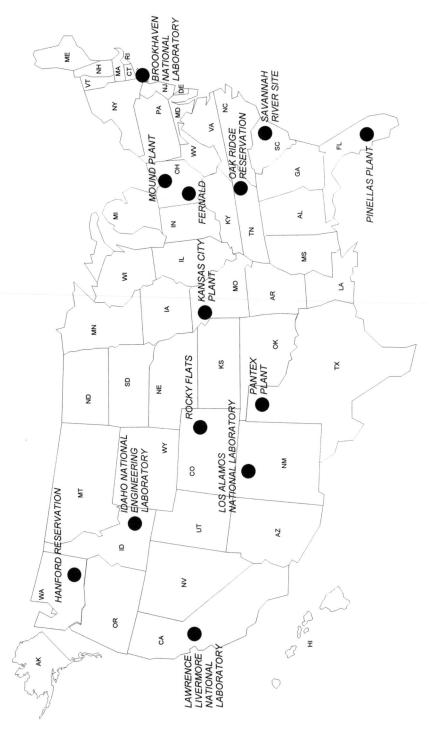

FIGURE 8.2 - CONTAMINATED NUCLEAR FACILITIES

By far, the chemical manufacturing industry generates the largest amount of hazardous waste in the United States. However, every industry generates huge quantities of hazardous wastes. Steel, paint, textiles, paper, automotive, electronics, transportation, utilities, plastics, furniture, printing, agricultural, mining, pharmaceuticals and petroleum refining industries – all produce, use and dispose of massive amounts of toxic materials. The disposal methods, quantities, and level of toxicity of chemicals released to the environment (via air, land, underground, surface water and transfers) vary widely by industry. Table 8.1 lists the top ten industries for toxic chemical releases in 1990.

TABLE 8.1 - Industrial Toxic Chemical Releases
(in thousands of pounds – 1990)

Industry	Air Releases	Surface Water	Underground Injection	Land Releases	Transfers	Total Pounds
Chemicals	695,358	133,479	658,662	98,518	251,193	2,107,156
Metals	351,509	12,501	20,052	315,591	364,125	1,081,447
Paper	243,936	37,676	0.07	7,368	18,441	359,510
Transportation	193,522	235	0.32	1,949	39,537	244,941
Plastics	192,541	463	15	200	22,455	224,534
Petroleum	71,299	4,987	37,851	3,114	9,249	134,214
Electrical	81,867	416	19	2,736	35,119	132,656
Food	26,886	5,404	36	8,689	9,116	92,393
Machinery	52,777	209	0.568	139	13,564	69,427
Furniture	60,051	4	0.07	7,368	4,328	64,796

Source: Adapted from Environmental Almanac, 1993 p.188. Data from USEPA, 1990 Toxics Release Inventory: Public Data Release (1992) Table 17, p. 58.

CONSIDER THE SOURCE

When assessing the threat to a residential community presented by a particular type of industry, you must initially evaluate the possible avenues of exposure. For example, residential areas that are downwind from industries that release significant quantities of toxics to the air would be of more concern than areas downwind of industries that have minimal airborne releases.

Communities that rely on surface water supplies as sources of drinking water and/or for recreation would have higher concerns about industries in an area that discharges wastes to streams and other surface waters. Conversely, homes and municipalities that rely on private and municipal wells for drinking water would need to assess the increased risk of industries that use underground storage and/or disposal. Communities near major transportation routes should have concerns about industries that transfer large quantities of toxic chemicals and wastes.

An evaluation of the hazards associated with the type of industry in a particular community also needs to consider the types of waste and how it is stored. It may be a case of quality versus quantity. Although one type of industry may discharge far higher quantities of toxic chemicals, small amounts of certain hazardous materials in the air or groundwater may represent a much greater health threat.

COMMUNITY RIGHT TO KNOW

In the mid-1980s, the public did get a "peek over the fence" in our ability to find out what types of chemicals are being used and released by companies in our neighborhoods. The Superfund Amendments and Reauthorization Act (SARA Title III) Emergency Planning and Community Right-to-Know requires companies to inventory their toxic materials and to report releases.

This act provides emergency workers and environmental agencies with detailed information on the types, quantities, and storage locations of hazardous materials at industrial and manufacturing sites. This information greatly assists groups, such as fire departments, who need to know what they could be dealing with during accidents, fires, or other catastrophes at industrial facilities.

The Community Right-to-Know Act also provided the public with the ability to access database information to determine what toxics may be in your backyard. The data can be used to compare the potential toxicity of the types of industry based in your community. Table 8.2 ranks each State in decreasing order for toxic chemical releases in 1990. Figure 8.3 indicates the numbers of waste disposal and treatment or storage facilities across the United States.

SUPERFUND

Hazardous material use, storage, and disposal areas exist in all fifty states. Of particular concern are active and abandoned illegal dumpsites. These sites are often little more than holes in the ground with none of the safeguards of modern landfills and other acceptable disposal sites. Illegal dumps typically have little or no record of the materials deposited and the result is a toxic stew. These extensively contaminated properties often come to light only when the toxic effects are felt by the public and investigations are subsequently conducted to trace the source.

In 1980, the Comprehensive Environmental Response, Compensation, and Liability Act (CERCLA) established the Superfund to address seriously contaminated properties. Unfortunately, decades of indiscriminate discharges, improper waste dumping, and bankrupt or abandoned facilities resulted in thousands of sites across the United States that are so contaminated that they are placed on a National Priorities List (NPL).

The NPL includes those sites that, based on EPA rankings, represent the greatest health threat to the public. A high level of threat is based on either the type of contamination or a high potential for exposure of the public to the contaminants. The fact is that it often takes the public's exposure to the toxic materials to discover a previously unknown hazardous site.

TABLE 8.2 - Toxic Releases by State - 1990

State	Tons (thousands)	State	Tons (thousands)
Louisiana	213.7	Kentucky	21.2
Texas	209.4	Washington	20.7
Tennessee	103.7	Iowa	20.3
Indiana	84.4	West Virginia	19.1
Ohio	84.2	Oklahoma	16.6
Utah	62.7	New Mexico	16.3
North Carolina	62.0	New Jersey	13.0
Michigan	59.9	Oregon	11.3
Illinois	59.5	Connecticut	10.7
Alabama	56.3	Massachusetts	10.4
Florida	53.3	Alaska	10.3
Mississippi	51.8	Nebraska	8.7
California	48.5	Maryland	8.0
Kansas	44.9	Maine	7.4
Pennsylvania	44.7	Wyoming	5.8
Virginia	39.8	Idaho	5.8
Georgia	38.9	New Hampshire	4.1
Arizona	36.0	Colorado	3.7
Missouri	34.3	Delaware	3.3
South Carolina	33.6	Rhode Island	2.6
New York	30.2	Nevada	1.6
Arkansas	28.9	South Dakota	1.5
Minnesota	26.0	North Dakota	1.1
Wisconsin	22.5	Vermont	0.5
Montana	21.3	Hawaii	0.4

Source: Adapted from Environmental Almanac, 1993 p.223. Data from USEPA, 1990 Toxics Release Inventory: Public Data Release (May 1992)

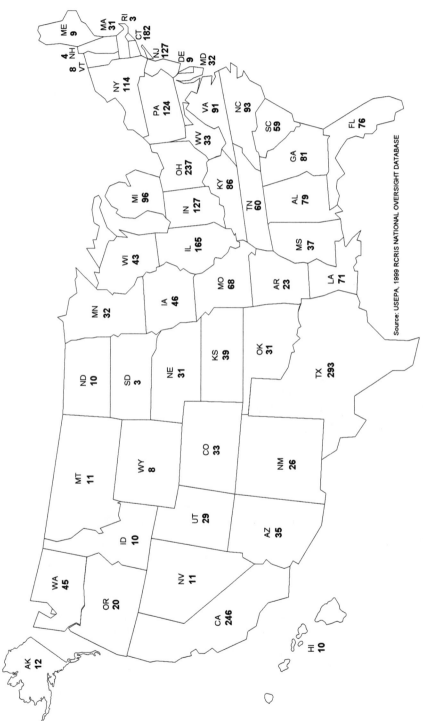

FIGURE 8.3 - NUMBER OF HAZARDOUS WASTE TREATMENT, STORAGE, AND DISPOSAL FACILITIES (March 1999)

Source: USEPA, 1999 RCRIS NATIONAL OVERSIGHT DATABASE

SLOW PROGRESS

In early 1998, approximately 1,200 sites were on the National Priorities List; new sites are added each year. When the parties responsible for the contamination cannot be located or are bankrupt, public funds are relied on to finance the remediation. Sadly, much of the money is spent over legal wrangling regarding responsibility rather than actual cleanup.

The Superfund was established in 1980 with $1.6 billion in appropriations. By 1990, over $6 billion had been spent and only fifty-two sites across the United States had been cleaned up. By the mid-1990s, the number of remediations had risen to approximately 250 sites with an additional 250 sites cleaned up in the later half of the decade. The relatively rapid increase in site completions is a result of the many years spent on the legal arguments and the extensive investigation phases to prepare the sites for remediation.

Because Superfund sites typically are the most hazardous known contamination in the country, remediation is almost always a lengthy process, often taking decades to achieve acceptable cleanup levels. Upon identification of a hazardous site, emergency action is typically taken to address obvious threats such as leaking storage systems or contaminated drinking water supplies. This is followed by a series of soil, groundwater and air quality investigations to provide a complete characterization of the problems.

Preliminary research into what may have gone where and physical investigations of abandoned sites can take years just to fully identify the types of contamination, what portions of the environment are affected, the extent of migration, and the potential health impact to the public and the environment. Several more years can pass during the study, development, modeling, testing and initial construction of an appropriate cleanup method.

Though Superfund sites may represent the worst of the worst, you can take some comfort from the fact that at least the sites have been identified. A devil known is certainly better than one that is not. Although Superfund sites exist across the United States, they are generally more prevalent in the heavily industrialized and populated states such as California, Florida, New Jersey,

New York and Pennsylvania. Figures 8.4 and 8.5 illustrate the total number of NPL sites per state and the total number of remedial completions per state, respectively.

GETTING THE LOWDOWN

For any Superfund site, EPA databases can be accessed to give complete descriptions of property locations, contaminants, portions of the environment affected and the remediation progress. Living in a community that includes Superfund sites will naturally raise a homeowner's level of concern. Fortunately, at least some information is available to make informed choices about the hazards that may be nearby. The sites that have yet to be discovered are the ones that eventually may be found the hard way - such as after drinking water becomes contaminated or there is the identification of a disease cluster.

An increased awareness of what to look for can go a long way toward identifying and perhaps preventing future Superfunds or other contaminated sites. Look for uncontrolled discharges into streams or lakes in a community. Check with local regulatory agencies to see if industries are typically in compliance with their disposal and discharge monitoring requirements. Evaluate the housekeeping practices of local industry – are materials stored haphazardly or is there evidence of improper disposal or burial activities? Pay attention to and report any "midnight dumpers". If concerns exist about the industry in an area, a little common sense and open eyes can answer many questions. Chapter 12 discusses further methods to more fully investigate suspect properties.

SOURCE OF DATA: USEPA, APRIL 1999

FIGURE 8.4 - NUMBER OF SUPERFUND SITES (APRIL 1999)

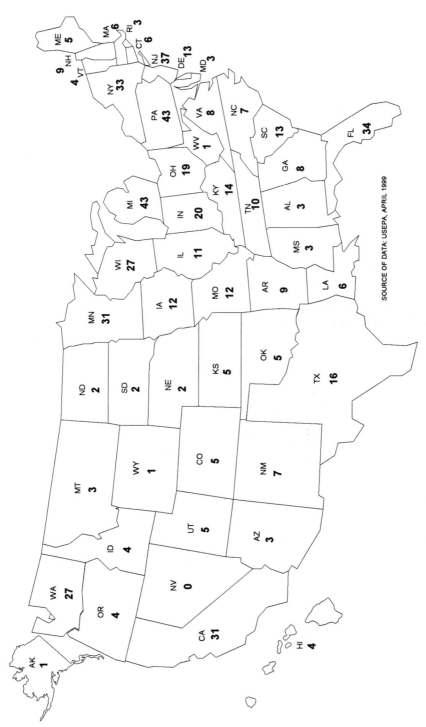

SOURCE OF DATA: USEPA, APRIL 1999

FIGURE 8.5 - NUMBER OF SUPERFUND SITE CONSTRUCTION COMPLETIONS (APRIL 1999)

DRINKING WATER

"When water chokes you, what are you to drink to wash it down?"

Aristotle

"Don't drink the water."

Friendly advice

WATER WATER EVERYWHERE

While our potential for exposure to environmental hazards in and around our homes varies considerably based in part on our lifestyles, choice of home, construction materials, socioeconomic status, area of the country, and even dumb luck, one common potential exposure is that we all drink water.

As our not too distant past of indiscriminant use, discharge, storage and disposal of hazardous materials has caught up with us, we have found that our drinking water supplies are most vulnerable to contamination. In those instances when our drinking water becomes degraded by the introduction of contaminants, the water then serves as a primary pathway for the direct ingestion of, and thereby, exposure to a multitude of pollutants.

Manmade chemical compounds and other natural contaminants are often persistent in the subsurface and can frequently migrate with relative ease through the environment. Once water supplies are impacted, it often takes years or even decades to restore the water to potable quality. Restoration, however, is frequently not economically or technologically feasible. Therefore, large portions of industrial and commercial areas in almost every state are routinely considered "beyond repair" and groundwater and surface water quality is seriously, and sometimes permanently, compromised.

Of course, contaminant problems extend well beyond industrial and disposal areas. Because pollutants vary in form as well as source, you can not assume that your water supply is immune from contamination just because you live in the suburbs. Problems with water quality can cover a broad spectrum - from simple objectionable tastes to cancer causing pollutants.

Over the past thirty years, the number of public and private water supply systems rendered non-potable has dramatically increased. Contamination sources range from agricultural runoff to industrial discharges, and from golf course and backyard pesticides/herbicides to underground tanks. Of course, the earth itself can be the source for many natural pollutants. Unfortunately, the discovery of many quality problems occurs only after they have developed. It is similar to finding your house is on fire. The key in both cases is prevention.

PRIVATE AND PUBLIC

In the immediate sense, our source of water in our home comes through one of two types of systems. Almost all residential water supplies are served by a public or private distribution system. When we assess the quality of our water supply, however, we must look beyond the tap and the distribution system and consider the origin of the water.

Public water supplies typically serve a large number of customers and are managed by either private water companies or municipalities. Public supplies derive their water from surface water, or groundwater, or a combination of both. Private water systems are most commonly represented by solitary wells that pump groundwater to serve individual residences. Both public and private systems are susceptible to contaminant problems and there are concerns specific to each supply system. The benefits and drawbacks associated with each of the supply sources are explored later in this chapter.

With the increase in environmental contamination and the resulting water quality problems, public systems have rightly been forced to increase the scope and frequency of supply monitoring. At least some form of pollutants exist in nearly all water, and there is a constant threat of new contaminants entering water supplies. Unfortunately, private well systems rarely undergo quality testing beyond the original installation period.

In some circumstances, the correction of water quality problems range from doing nothing, and allowing time and dilution to be the solution, to converting to alternate water sources (bottled water, new wells, switching to public supplies). Somewhere in between are an assortment of treatment methods designed to reduce and remove specific contaminants from a water supply.

The treatment for contaminated water may be implemented on a large scale in association with a public distribution system, or on a significantly smaller scale at the tap in your home. Regardless of the approach to correcting a water quality problem, it is important to remember that the original source of the problem also needs to be identified and eliminated. Unless the source of pollutants is found and corrected, the need to treat the water supply can become virtually permanent.

IS IT SAFE?

Is it okay to drink the water? In most cases and in most areas of the United States, the answer is yes. In fact, as a whole the U.S. has one of the safest and most closely monitored water supplies in the world. Nevertheless, given our level of industrialization and expanding population, pollutants do migrate, accidents do happen, and water supplies are increasingly rendered unfit to drink.

In April 1993, a bacterium known as cryptosporidium made it through treatment systems in the public water supply for Milwaukee, Wisconsin. As a result of drinking the contaminated water, thousands of people became seriously ill and dozens died. Although this case was extreme in the outcome, contaminant problems due to chemicals and bacteria are not rare. Pollutants commonly slip through treatment processes, especially when the contaminants are not anticipated. Every day in every state, water supplies become unexpectedly contaminated by leaks from underground tanks, surface runoff from roads, migration of buried wastes, and overuse of pesticides, fertilizers, and herbicides.

Not all water is created equal. Water exists in a number of forms, at greatly differing levels of quality, and in a number of environments. We can ordinarily find water as snow, ice, fog, or, of course, as a liquid. Because of the nature of water as a "universal solvent", even pure water in pristine lakes and streams contains dissolved organic and inorganic substances. Groundwater taken from anywhere can have high levels of dissolved minerals and other substances that naturally occur in the earth. As water passes through a never-ending cycle, contaminants, both natural and manmade, are incorporated. The concentrations can be almost non-detectable. Alternatively, you may find extreme cases where several feet of petroleum may be floating on the water table.

GETTING IT FROM THE SOURCE

Where does your water come from? No, the faucet is not the complete answer. An understanding of the water (hydrologic) cycle provides an appreciation of the vulnerability to contamination of our most vital natural resource. Most water that is collected and distributed to homes originates from surface water sources (streams, lakes, and reservoirs) or from groundwater (the water found in soil and rock beneath the ground surface).

Groundwater is not a vast, open reservoir or river that flows just beneath the ground surface. Instead, groundwater exists at variable depths in small pores between soil grains and in fractures in rocks that are completely saturated with water. The top of this zone of saturation is called the water table. It can intersect with the ground surface, as in the case of some springs, or it can exist at great depth. We pump groundwater from geologic formations called aquifers. An aquifer typically consists of a layer or layers of sandy and/or gravelly material or even fractured rock that can yield sustainable quantities of water.

Most of the groundwater in the United States originates from precipitation that migrates downward through soil and rock. Surface water in streams and lakes that "leak" to the underlying soils also contribute to groundwater. It is always in motion, although not in the sense of open flow like in a river. Instead, groundwater moves very slowly through the interconnections of the pore spaces in soil and through joined fractures in rock.

Under certain geologic conditions, the natural rate of groundwater flow can be as slow as a number of inches per decade (such as through clay) and as rapid as several feet per day (such as through highly fractured or cavernous rock). Most wells extract water from the ground through perforated casing or open holes that are mechanically drilled into aquifers. A pumping mechanism with intake and discharge piping is installed either at the bottom or at the top of the well to extract water that flows into the casing.

Not too long ago, when water was more abundant and less likely to become contaminated, wells often were dug by hand. Today, it is usually necessary to drill much deeper to find sufficient water. Drilling to greater depths is also necessary to have an adequate soil buffer to minimize the chance that surface contamination will enter the groundwater and well. Figure 9.1 is a simplified, cross-section depiction of the components of a typical groundwater production well.

Most large, public systems obtain their water from surface sources. Smaller public systems, which may serve as few as twenty-five household

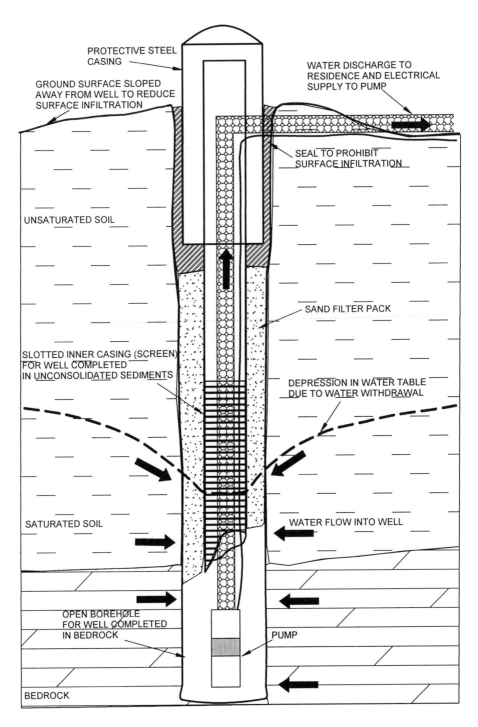

FIGURE 9.1 - CROSS SECTION OF TYPICAL GROUNDWATER WELL

connections, tend to use groundwater as their primary source. When private wells are factored in, approximately one-half of the population of the United States receives its water supply from groundwater. Withdrawal of the water at rates faster than it is replenished in the aquifer results in the local and possibly regional lowering of the water table. As a consequence, wells can go dry – typically beginning with the shallowest. This problem is exacerbated during drought periods when groundwater use is up and precipitation is down.

A NEVER ENDING CYCLE

Gravity governs the direction of groundwater flow because a water table has at least some gradient (slope) and, of course, water naturally flows downhill. In general, the direction of groundwater flow will be a subdued reflection of the surface of the ground. It is important to recognize, however, that pumping from a well creates a variable zone in the aquifer that pulls water toward the well. Pumping from the well can greatly accelerate underground movement of water and alter or even reverse the natural flow direction and slope of the water table.

The amount of water in the atmosphere, on the earth in oceans, lakes, streams, vegetation, and ice, and within the earth, is for the most part a constant volume - it is only the form that changes. Figure 9.2 illustrates the hydrologic cycle and the ways that water is stored in and moves through our environment.

AND NOT A DROP TO DRINK

Contamination of surface or groundwater supplies results from manmade pollutants or natural materials that can be classified into one of four categories. Contaminants can be chemical (organic and inorganic), physical, bacteriological, or radioactive. All can affect our lives in ways that range from minor inconveniences to serious illnesses and poisoning. Water within the hydrologic cycle encounters and incorporates these contaminants in the atmosphere, in bodies of water, or in the ground.

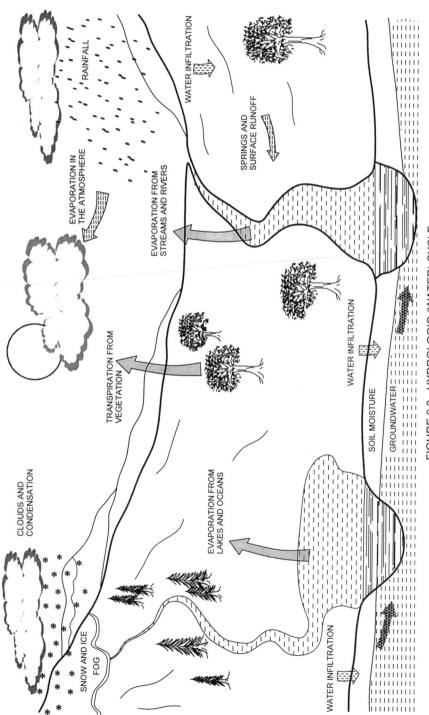

FIGURE 9.2 - HYDROLOGIC (WATER) CYCLE

Fortunately, natural processes like sunlight, oxygen, evaporation, and bacteriological action, can significantly reduce the levels and toxicity of contaminants. Depending on the type and quantity of pollutant and the location of the release, the ground can be a natural filter and absorb much of a discharge before it gets to a water supply.

The ground, acting as a filter, is the principle behind most residential septic disposal systems where wastewater from a home is dispersed into a leachfield and allowed to seep through soil. However, the basic fact of all filters (including the ground) is that they have a finite capacity. At some point, either because of limited filter area or excessive contaminant loading, the filter medium (in this case the soil) cannot absorb additional contaminants. The result will usually be groundwater contamination, either by liquid pollutants directly reaching the water table and/or by pollutants being carried in solution as precipitation percolates downward. This set of circumstances occurs not only with septic systems, but also with leaking storage tanks, landfill leachate, underground and aboveground industrial discharges, settling lagoons, dry wells, etc.

POLLUTANT SOURCES

Because groundwater flow directions can vary and because the zone of groundwater capture around a well can be expansive, it is important to consider the potential for contaminant sources from all directions – not just upslope along the water table. Under certain conditions, pumping from a well can alter natural flow directions that are hundreds and even thousands of feet away. The result is that a well may draw contaminants that originated from a leaking tank or other source as much as a half-mile away. Near coastal areas, excessive groundwater withdrawal can result in saltwater intrusions (the upwelling of underlying, denser saltwater). That can produce brackish and saline water that is unfit to drink.

Surface water bodies do not have the natural soil buffer usually associated with groundwater. Because contaminants are often discharged in their raw form directly into surface water, it is significantly more susceptible to pollution than groundwater. Unfortunately, not all groundwater has a buffer of soil above it. Fractured rock, exposed at the ground surface, may serve as a direct pathway for contaminants to enter deep bedrock aquifers.

Roadway runoff contains petroleum, metals, and road salt. Ground surface runoff may include industrial chemicals and petroleum as well as pesticides and herbicides that directly enter drainage channels, streams, and rivers. Although golf courses may look pretty, the looks have a price. They are a major source of chemical runoff. Accidental and intentional dumping of hazardous materials such as spent chemicals and waste oil often go straight into waterways. Wastewater treatment facilities routinely discharge partially treated septic and other wastes into streams and rivers. Although by no means complete, some of the most common sources of water contamination are listed below:

- ➢ Septic wastes
- ➢ Agricultural animal waste runoff
- ➢ Landfills, waste disposal
- ➢ Leaking tanks and pipelines
- ➢ Industrial chemical releases
- ➢ Acid rain, acid mine drainage
- ➢ Fertilizers
- ➢ Pesticides and herbicides
- ➢ Salt water intrusions
- ➢ Road runoff

Figure 9.3 illustrates some of the many ways that contaminants can enter the hydrologic cycle.

COMMON WATER QUALITY CONCERNS

Fortunately, most of the water quality problems for homeowners are related to nuisance and aesthetic issues such as hardness, odor, color, or objectionable tastes, which (in the majority of cases) come from natural influences. Because wells are drilled into the earth, groundwater can also be

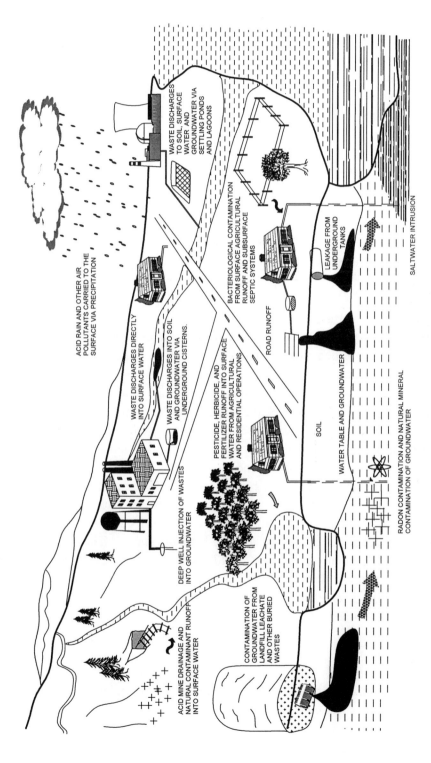

FIGURE 9.3 - CONTAMINANT ENTRY INTO THE HYDROLOGIC CYCLE

contaminated by another naturally occurring condition - radon. Exposure to radon tainted water in your home can occur through showering or other typical household uses that aerate the water. The radon can then be inhaled. See Chapter 4 for a more detailed discussion of radon risks in your home.

After initial well construction and potability testing of private well supplies, the burden of any future testing for pollutants falls on the homeowner. Most homeowners are typically unaware of the relative ease with which contaminants can seep into their well water. Even when homeowners are aware of the possibility of contamination, they may be unaware of the best way to investigate and what specific tests are appropriate. Alternatively, they may be unwilling to take the trouble and often considerable expense associated with periodic sampling and laboratory analyses.

Increasingly, we find man-made contaminants in water supplies that cause much more serious concerns than common aesthetic problems. When present even in miniscule quantities, certain chemicals have such extreme toxicity that they render entire water supplies hazardous. As is the case with most environmental hazards, we have found that children, older people, and people who are ill are the most susceptible to pollutants in drinking water.

With respect to public water supplies, the Federal Safe Drinking Water Act (SDWA) was passed in 1974, and was designed to ensure safe supplies of water. Components of the act banned the use of lead in plumbing, required protection of water sources, and accelerated EPA regulations. The SDWA also requires public systems to monitor their water quality regularly and to conduct routine analyses for specific contaminants. The EPA has set Maximum Contaminant Levels (MCLs) for approximately 100 different pollutants that are allowed to be in drinking water. Individual states may set levels that are stricter than the MCLs, but they cannot be more lenient.

MONITORING

Each year, there are unfortunately thousands of violations of the Safe Drinking Water Act by public suppliers. However, it is important to note that many of the violations are the result of paperwork and monitoring-schedule issues and are not actual water quality violations. Compliance with the SDWA represents a considerable economic burden for municipalities and water companies. As a result, smaller public systems are often exempt from certain regulations because of the economic hardship. The exemptions represent an increased risk to water quality.

Community notifications are required when a public system fails to comply with the drinking water standards. Just as compliance failures range from simple reporting problems to violations of water quality standards – the level of public notification varies from notices in the newspaper to direct announcements through the mail and electronic media. A violation of the maximum contaminant levels requires notification of those served by the system within twenty-four hours. Customer notification is supposed to include information about the health risks, measures being taken by the system to correct the problem, and what the user may need to do regarding alternative water supplies until the situation is rectified.

Because of the type of community or the presumed protected source of water, some of the testing of public and private systems may appear to be overkill. For instance, you would not expect to find industrial solvents in a water supply system for rural areas. However, because a little pollutant can go such a long way toward contamination, the testing is prudent.

Additionally, we increasingly find smaller-scale industry interspersed in our suburban and rural areas. Consequently, significant sources of pollutant discharges exist where it may have been presumed that the sources of water were relatively protected. Less densely populated areas are also often used as landfill and disposal sites, where virtually infinite quantities of contaminants have been placed in areas that may otherwise have comparatively safe water. I am familiar with a number of groundwater contamination cases due to industry and disposal in suburban and rural areas. Many of these cases required the shutdown of private and municipal wells, conversion to alternate supplies, and installation of various treatment technologies to reduce contaminant levels.

THE HEALTH EFFECTS

Sadly, consuming water contaminated with "acceptable" levels of manmade contaminants has become the norm. In most cases, the contamination of a water supply is due to low concentrations of chemicals or other substances that are transient or do not represent significant health threats. Provided that the contaminant is not consumed over an extended period, in most cases there is no lasting effect.

However, what level is acceptable depends entirely on the toxicity of a contaminant. Some chemicals are just so dangerous; they are not safe at any level in our water. Allowable limits for some highly hazardous chemicals (such as chlordane - an insecticide) are as low as our ability to reliably detect the contaminant in laboratory analyses. Allowable concentrations of dioxin are tens of millions of times less than some other hazardous chemicals such as those found in gasoline. Other contaminant limits are significantly higher – based typically on animal, human, and epidemiological studies that try to estimate exposures and acceptable cancer risks along with the rates of other diseases.

The EPA establishes maximum contaminant levels through a risk-assessment process.   Cancer-related assessments are determined by exposures to contaminants that may increase the risk of cancer by one in one million over a seventy-year lifespan.   This also presumes the somewhat generous consumption of two liters of the contaminated water per day. The maximum levels for other non-cancer causing pollutants are set at values below which there is no adverse effect. Fortunately, or unfortunately, depending on how you see it, a relatively small number of studies conclusively demonstrate the effects of long-term contaminant exposures on humans.

SHORT TERM - LONG TERM

The potential for damage to the health of an individual, and the severity of the damage, are directly related to a person's susceptibility, the length of exposure, and the toxicity and concentration of water contaminants. In the case of nitrates, pathogens (certain bacteria and viruses) and some rare chemicals, the health effects can be relatively immediate and severe. For example, elevated levels of nitrates in water can produce an anemic condition known as "blue baby syndrome" where the oxygen carrying capacity in an infant's blood is dangerously reduced. Because of this, pregnant or nursing mothers should take special care to avoid water contaminated with nitrates.

Despite some notable exceptions (such as a bacterium that caused widespread illness and deaths in Wisconsin), the required monitoring of public water quality generally prevents gross exposures. Short-term exposures to some high levels of contaminants can cause acute health effects such as vomiting, skin disorders and in rare instances death. However, it is more likely that we would be exposed to lower concentrations of contaminants.

The low-level pollutants may exist below the ability of a laboratory to detect them or routine screening may not even test for some pollutants. These contaminants, ingested over time, can have more chronic impacts such as birth defects, organ disorders and cancer. Table 9.1 summarizes some of the most common water contaminants, allowable concentrations, the possible sources and the potential health effects.

WHERE TO DRINK

Virtually nowhere in the United States can claim to have water that is without risk of contamination – even bears take care of their business in the woods. Although certain locations and cases occasionally dominate the headlines, all communities can suffer from water quality problems that are both natural and manmade.

From the suburbs of Minneapolis, to irrigated croplands in Texas, to the known and unknown "Love Canals" throughout the United States, water supplies are in constant threat of contamination due to what we make, how we use it, how we store it, where we discharge it, how we grow it, how we kill it, and where we bury it.

TABLE 9.1 - National Primary Drinking Water Standards for Common Pollutants, Potential Contaminant Sources, and Possible Health Effects

Contaminant	Maximum Contaminant Level* (mg/l)	Potential Sources	Potential Health Effects
Benzene	0.005	gasoline, plastics manufacturing, detergent and adhesive manufacturing	cancer
Ethylbenzene	0.7	gasoline, chemical manufacturing	liver, kidney, and nervous system
Toluene	1.0	gasoline, manufacturing solvent, paint and lacquer manufacturing	liver, kidney, nervous, and circulatory systems.
Tetrachloroethylene	0.005	solvent, textile manufacturing, drycleaning	cancer
Trichloroethylene	0.005	degreaser, textile and adhesive manufacturing	cancer
Xylenes	10.0	gasoline, paints, inks, detergents manufacturing	liver, kidney, and nervous system
Coliform (total)	<5% samples	human and animal fecal waste septic systems	digestive disorders (indicator)
Giardia Lamblia	treatment	human and animal fecal waste	digestive disorders
Legionella	treatment	natural waters, heating and cooling systems, standing water	Legionnaire's disease
Viruses	treatment	human and animal fecal waste	digestive disorders
Arsenic	0.05	natural deposits, electronics, pesticides, metal manufacturing	skin and nervous system disorders
Beryllium	0.004	electrical, aerospace, defense industries	bone, lung damage
Copper	1.3	preservative, natural deposits, plumbing, electronics	gastrointestinal irritation
Cyanide	0.2	electroplating, steel, printing, plastics industries	thyroid, nervous system damage
Lead	0.015	natural, industrial waste, plumbing	kidneys, nervous system damage
Mercury	0.002	natural, batteries, electronics, runoff	kidneys, nervous system damage
Nitrate	10.0	animal and sewage waste, fertilizer, natural deposits	methemoglobulinemia
Alachlor	0.002	agricultural herbicide runoff	cancer
Carbofuran	0.04	agricultural runoff	nervous, reproductive systems
Chlordane	0.002	insecticide runoff	cancer
2,4-D	0.07	agricultural, recreational, residential herbicide runoff	liver, kidney damage
Dioxin	0.00000003	herbicides, chemical production byproduct	cancer
Lindane	0.0002	agricultural, residential, lumber insecticide	liver, kidney, immune system, circulatory system
PCB's	0.0005	alloy & electrical manufacturing, transformers, plasticizers	cancer
Radium 226/228	5 pCi/L	natural deposits	cancer

* - Individual state standards may be more strict. (mg/l = milligrams per liter, parts per million)
Adapted from USEPA Publication 815-K-97002, July 1997, p.18

For example:

➢ Long Island, NY – groundwater wells were contaminated with pesticide used in former potato fields.

➢ Fernald Superfund Site, OH – surface and groundwater contamination due to chemical and radioactive materials.

➢ Mississippi River – carcinogenic pesticides found in water samples.

➢ St. Petersburg, FL – drinking water aquifer impacted by radioactive waste discharges.

➢ Montague, MI – improper management of chemical wastes contaminated fish, surface water, and groundwater.

➢ Seymour, IN – chemical wastes discharged directly into an aquifer.

ASSESS THE SOURCE

As a homeowner, the investigation of public or private water quality represents one of the most important issues when you are assessing the environmental quality of your home or community. Assuming there is a public water supplier, a review of local newspapers would disclose notices of violations. Information on water quality can also be obtained by requesting copies of testing reports directly from the water company or the municipality. Additional sources of information on public systems or groundwater quality include local health departments, state departments of environmental resources and protection, and regional offices of the U.S. Environmental Protection Agency.

Individual states are compiling data collected from public systems into overall reports on water quality. The EPA is summarizing these reports to develop comprehensive data on public water conditions throughout the United States. The public can access the reports on a state or federal level to assess general water quality in different portions of the country.

When evaluating the potential and actual water quality of a region, it is not sufficient to consider just the industrialization, or lack thereof. Therefore, when you are evaluating your water, consider that the water may flow from or may be piped in from an entirely separate region - which may be more or less susceptible to contamination. For example, the bulk of the public water supply for Wilmington, Delaware originates from surface water flowing from Pennsylvania. An additional example is water quality in New York City, New York, which is regularly considered to be very good. Of course, the water does not come from beneath Manhattan or from the Hudson River; it comes from protected watersheds and reservoirs located upstate.

Because groundwater and surface water vary significantly in quality and susceptibility to contamination, there are advantages and disadvantages to each as a water supply source. A homeowner or prospective homeowner must consider these factors in evaluating a place to live and the water supply that serves a home. Table 9.2 summarizes some of the advantages and disadvantages associated with both of the possible sources.

TO PROTECT AND TO SERVE

Before you purchase a home with a private well, conduct sampling and analyses of the water supply. In fact, many communities require water quality testing of wells before they will allow the transfer of residential real estate. The first step in water assessment is to simply smell it, look at it, and taste it. Regardless of whether contaminants are present, if the water is not aesthetically pleasing, no one wants to drink it. Naturally, by examining the water with your senses, there may be readily detectable characteristics such as a chemical odor or unusual colorings that may indicate problems that are more serious.

At a minimum, laboratory analyses of samples from the water supply should include nitrate, coliform, and lead. If there are indications that other contaminants are a reasonable possibility (e.g. petroleum odors from the water, with service-station tanks leaking just down the block,), analyses should be expanded to include compounds such as volatile organics and petroleum hydrocarbons. Depending on the types of analyses to be conducted, it may be appropriate to collect samples during different times of the day.

TABLE 9.2 - Comparison of Water Supply Sources

	Groundwater Source	Surface Water Source
Advantages	- natural filtration through the ground. - relatively constant quality. - relatively slow spread of contamination. - low sediment load.	- higher use by public suppliers, no homeowner responsibility for treatment and monitoring. - softer water. - "natural" cleansing of water due to dilution, sunlight, oxygen and evaporation.
Disadvantages	- dissolved minerals can be high (hard water). - contamination can be persistent and difficult to remediate. - potential for radon. - homeowner is responsible for monitoring of private well quality.	- more easily contaminated and contamination rapidly spreads. - susceptible to airborne contaminants. - more susceptible to drought conditions. - possibly higher sediment content/load.

To ensure the reliability of test results, use an independent party to collect the samples and a certified laboratory to analyze them. Local health departments may be able to assist in this regard as well as with the interpretation of the results. Most analytical laboratories and consultants can conduct the sampling, make sure proper technique is used, and subsequently interpret the test results. If the sampling and testing costs are split between a seller and a buyer, this can help to assure the impartiality of the analyses. Many private companies that sell water treatment equipment will also offer free water testing. The potential for biased findings in this situation should be obvious.

TAKING MEASURES

Table 9.3 summarizes many of suspect circumstances that can develop with public and private water supplies. Potential causes of the problems and the tests that are typically recommended to investigate the conditions are also specified.

When water testing identifies elevated contaminant levels or objectionable aesthetic problems, the first step to remember is not to panic. The next is to make absolutely sure of the results – re-test the water. Re-testing can verify whether the level of a contaminant is constant or if the first result was abnormal. Furthermore, laboratories can and do make mistakes not only in the identification of contaminants, but also in the measured concentrations. Cross-contamination in the laboratory can occur and sometimes more benign compounds can be falsely detected as a pollutant that should be of more concern. Re-testing may also be warranted if your concerns are not relieved by a first negative result and/or if the suspect conditions change or occur again. It may be prudent to have the second sampling and analyses performed by a different laboratory to serve as a crosscheck of the first.

If you have a water quality problem, the source must be identified and if possible, eliminated. If a public system services your household, contact your municipality and/or water company and perhaps even the health department to advise them of your findings and concerns. If your water source is a private well, most likely you will still want to contact the health department to obtain their advice. Information from the health department may also aid in finding out whether a particular pollutant is part of a larger regional problem and whether the source has already been identified.

TREATMENT MEASURES

When the source of aesthetic or other problems of contamination cannot be eliminated before the water comes into your home, you will need to consider changing the water source or installing a treatment system. Private wells that are significantly contaminated can seldom be cleaned up within a convenient

TABLE 9.3 - Water Quality Conditions and Concerns

Conditions and Health Concerns	Possible Common Causes	Recommended Analyses
Chemical odor or taste, (sweet/bitter) Paint thinner-like odor. Cancer, cancer clusters, liver, kidney, stomach disorders, leukemia.	Organic chemicals due to industrial waste discharges, dry cleaning solvents, landfills.	Volatile Organics
Petroleum odor or taste, rainbow sheen on water. Cancers, organ disorders.	Leakage from gasoline stations or heating oil tanks. Waste oil dumping	Volatile Organics Base/Neutral Organics Fuel additives
Sewage-like odor. Gastroenteric problems, cramping.	Septic waste entering water. Surface runoff entering well system. Animal waste.	Coliform Giardia Viruses
Blue-Baby Syndrome, asphyxia, bluish extremities, blue lips, labored breathing, unconsciousness.	Nitrate contamination due to fertilizers, sewage or animal waste.	Nitrate Coliform
Physical indications in water not obvious.	Agricultural, recreational, or residential overuse of herbicides and pesticides.	Herbicides Pesticides
Cancer, liver, kidney, stomach disorders.	Radionuclides (odorless and tasteless), nuclear waste.	Radon Gross activity
Appetite loss, joint pain, neurological problems, memory and concentration difficulties, kidney damage.	Natural or waste lead deposits, batteries, leaded gasoline. Lead piping and solder.	Lead
Reddish water, rust colored staining in sinks, toilets, and on clothing.	Natural iron and/or manganese.	Iron Manganese
Salty or bitter taste, briny, unpalatable taste.	Salt contamination due to road surface runoff (deicing) and/or saltwater intrusions.	Sodium Chloride Total Dissolved Solids
Rotten egg odor, corrosion of piping and fixtures.	Sewer gas, bacteria, naturally acidic water, pH reduction due to treatment systems.	Hydrogen Sulfide pH
Sediment in water, cloudy water. Hard water (soap and mineral scale)	Disturbances in piping and/or well system. Natural minerals.	Hardness

period. Depending on the type of pollutant, the only reasonable option may be to connect the home to a public water supply or to drill a new well. Evaluate with a professional whether drilling a new well would be an effective solution. You will need to consider the type of contamination, hydrogeology, and the potential for a new well to encounter the same problems.

If the treatment of a contaminated water supply is feasible, in most cases it will require expert consultation and expert service to design, install, and maintain a pollutant removal system. A treatment system will have to be tailored to the type and concentration of the contaminant, household water volume use, efficiency of contaminant removal, economics, ages and health of the users, and potential changes in household water use. Consideration must also be given to the fact that regular and expensive analytical testing may be necessary to evaluate the continued effectiveness of the treatment system and to detect unanticipated increases in the contaminant load.

Table 9.4 summarizes some of the many systems available for the treatment of water supplies. Point-of-use (POU) systems treat water at individual taps such as faucet filters or undersink systems. Point-of-entry (POE) systems are designed to treat the entire water supply before it is distributed through your home. Some of the treatment methods can be used in combination with others or perhaps modified as household needs and contaminant conditions dictate. Each option has limits of effectiveness and other drawbacks. Therefore, the applicability of a treatment system and the specifics of the contamination problem need to be carefully evaluated before choosing a treatment method.

Activated carbon filtration units are available in a variety of sizes and configurations to treat the entire household supply or as single faucet systems. Organic and other contaminants in the water adsorb onto the microscopic surfaces of granulated carbon in the filter. Over time, the efficiency of the carbon is reduced and must be replaced to maximize removal of the contaminants.

Filtration systems consist of paper, sand, ceramic, or other substances to mechanically strain the water stream. In most cases, mechanical filters are used to correct aesthetic problems. Solids that are larger than the pores of

TABLE 9.4 - Potential Treatment Systems for Common Water Quality Problems

Problem/ Contaminant	Activated Carbon Adsorption	Physical Filtration	Air Stripper	Chlorination	Ion Exchange	Reverse Osmosis	Ultraviolet Disinfection	Distillation
Organic Chemicals	POU POE		POE					
Radon	POE		POE					
Pesticides	POU POE					POU		
Bacteria		POU POE		POE			POE	POE
Sediment, Turbidity	POU POE	POU POE						
Iron	POU POE	POE	POE		POE			
Metals					POE	POU		POU POE
Nitrates						POU		POU POE
Taste	POU POE	POU						
Odor	POU POE							
Hard Water					POE	POU		

POU - Point of Use
POE - Point of Entry

the filter substance are screened out as they pass through the filter. Water flow rates will reduce as the filter medium becomes clogged, thereby requiring flushing, cleaning or replacement.

Air stripping units come in a variety of configurations for treating the entire household water supply. The technology relies on large volumes of air forced at high rates through contaminated water. Organic chemicals, which are volatile, are partitioned from the water as it passes through a medium that increases the surface area exposure of the contaminant. Operations and maintenance requirements can be high, and therefore, the systems are not commonly used in homes.

Chlorination kills bacteria. However, this type of system is typically not recommended for residential usage because the chemicals can be dangerous and the systems hard to maintain. Another drawback is that chlorination of water can actually increase the formation of and toxicity of previously existing pollutants (such as hydrocarbons and volatile organics).

Ion exchange treatment systems rely on the natural electrical charge of pollutants to remove them from the water; they are transferred electrically onto a replaceable medium. These systems usually treat the entire household supply. Manual and automatic units are available and are relatively simple to maintain.

Reverse osmosis units force water through a series of staged filters and membranes to remove primarily inorganic materials (metals, etc.). The systems require flushing of the pollutants to maintain efficiency. Some of the significant drawbacks are that these systems are usually very expensive to operate and waste significant amounts of water.

Ultraviolet disinfection systems pass water contaminated with pathogens through ultraviolet light, which kills the organisms. The ultraviolet light can be very effective unless the water is cloudy or has suspended material that shields the bacteria from the radiation. Because of this possibility, ultraviolet disinfection should be last when a series of treatment steps are necessary. An ultraviolet disinfection system is relatively simple to operate and maintain.

Distillation units boil the water supply and then condense the steam back into liquid. These systems are slow and expensive to operate and require considerable maintenance. Natural beneficial minerals may be lost from the drinking water because the minerals are not transferred into the steam during purification.

PREVENT

The problems associated with a contaminated water supply can be severe. Due to the maintenance, costs, and potential for undetected failures, treatment systems in the home should rarely be considered as permanent solutions for anything other than aesthetic problems.

Aside from the potentially devastating health effects associated with certain drinking water contaminants, the costs and inconvenience associated with purchasing bottled water, converting to an alternative water supply, installing and maintaining a treatment system, drilling a new well, or even moving, can be extreme. As the saying goes, "an ounce of prevention is worth a pound of cure".

➢Do whatever it takes to make sure you don't contribute potential contaminants to surface or groundwater.
➢Don't discharge waste oil, paints, anti-freeze, or other hazardous materials onto the ground surface, into storms sewers, or into water bodies. Take hazardous materials to authorized disposal or recycling facilities.
➢Limit your use of pesticides, herbicides, and fertilizers.
➢Don't put hazardous substances into your septic system. Take the materials to authorized disposal facilities.
➢Maintain and repair surface components of a private well system to prohibit surface runoff from infiltrating.
➢Locate wells hydraulically and topographically upslope from septic systems. Ensure septic systems are working properly and are not overloaded.

➢Periodically conduct water supply sampling and analytical testing for parameters of concern.

➢Use only licensed well drillers and plumbers for work on wells and water systems.

STORAGE TANKS

"Something is rotten in the state of Denmark."

William Shakespeare

WHAT IS THAT TICKING?

Storage tanks, especially underground storage tanks, are analogous to ticking time bombs. Practically universal in our communities, storage tanks contain everything from heating oil to gasoline, from manufacturing chemicals to hazardous wastes. The problem is that the almost routine spills and leaks from storage tanks present a tremendous source of air quality concerns, potential explosive hazards, and perhaps of greatest concern, soil and groundwater contamination plumes that often impact drinking water.

Homeowners can encounter the problems of discharges firsthand, either when a leaking tank in their community degrades the environment, or when the heating oil supply tank for their residence leaks. If you are buying a house, the integrity and location of a tank is of considerable importance.

Common tank sizes used for all purposes, range from 250 gallons to 20,000 gallons in capacity. The Environmental Protection Agency estimates we have more than three million underground storage tanks in the United States. However, tens of thousands of additional tanks likely exist, but are not included in official tallies. The numbers of tanks are almost assuredly underestimated because they are found on abandoned properties, because owners ignored laws and the tanks were never properly registered, or because certain tanks are exempt from registration programs. Although hundreds of tanks are removed from service every day because they are obsolete or due to environmental regulations, thousands more should be investigated and removed.

Since fuel oil replaced coal furnaces and fireplaces as the primary means for heating buildings, storage tanks have been in widespread use for most of the past century. Heating oil tanks service residential, commercial, educational, manufacturing, religious, military, governmental, medical, and almost every other type of property.

Tanks are also widely used for motor fuels such as diesel and gasoline at service stations, airports, bus depots, warehouses, municipal garages, and farms, as well as for emergency generators that can be located anywhere. Transportation and vehicle maintenance facilities also typically include tanks to store waste products such as used motor oil and anti-freeze. Many motor fuel categories of tanks were installed as a hedge against the petroleum shortages of the 1970s. Unfortunately, a great number of these tanks have reached the limits of their useful life.

Although storage tanks are virtually universal in our country, some localities have significantly fewer than others do. Warmer climates have a reduced need for heating and the number of heating oil tanks is correspondingly reduced. Additionally, some portions of the country rely more heavily on natural gas, propane, or electricity for heating and the number of oil tanks is less in these areas. Communities that are isolated from industry and commercial zones will also have fewer tanks.

REGULATION

Just like the 55-gallon drum, tanks are commonly utilized to contain hazardous chemicals and wastes. They are present at most manufacturing facilities and at many controlled and uncontrolled waste sites. Most storage tanks are constructed from steel and were installed long before regulations for corrosion protection, spill prevention, and leak detection were put into place in an effort to mitigate contaminant releases. Many other tanks are constructed from fiberglass reinforced plastic, which, although it does not corrode, can be highly susceptible to damage from improper installation and maintenance.

Leaks and spills from storage tank systems represent a serious threat to drinking water and the environment in general. Because of this threat, in 1986 the EPA passed regulations concerning the operation of underground storage tank systems. Most states followed with their own laws that are at least as strict as the federal regulations. The intent is to prevent discharges from occurring in the first place, or if a leak does occur to detect discharges before significant damage is done.

In general, facilities with tanks that are regulated based on size, contents, or usage are required to upgrade their tanks with discharge safeguards or remove them from service. Because of the overwhelming number of tanks in the United States, it has taken more than fourteen years to phase in the regulations. Despite the fact that all tanks can rust, residential tanks (including large tanks used for apartment buildings) are exempt from nearly all of the regulations – unless a discharge to the environment has been confirmed.

The exemption for residential tanks is not because they are any better maintained or less likely to leak, but rather because homeowners commonly do not have the financial resources necessary to comply with the requirements to upgrade or replace tank systems. In addition, the qualified consulting and contracting industry is not large enough to handle the vast number of residential tanks together with all other regulated tanks.

WHAT IS THE PROBLEM?

Although aboveground and underground tanks both contain hazardous materials, aboveground tanks are generally of less concern. Because they are exposed at the ground surface, aboveground tanks are easily inspected for problems and are much less subject to the corrosion that causes the majority of leaks in buried tank systems.

Whether or not an underground tank is leaking now, the one sure guarantee is that bare steel will corrode and leak eventually. My experience indicates that approximately one-quarter to one-third of all underground tank systems have moderate to severe discharges. The discharges from storage systems occur most often as leaks from the tank and associated piping (due to corrosion and loose fittings), or due to improper installation.

Additional problems occur during product delivery when fuel is spilled or the tank is inadvertently overfilled and contamination results around the fill neck of the tank. Improper activities by tank operators can also accelerate leaks. In the case of gasoline tanks, for years it had been a common practice to drop measuring sticks to the bottom of tanks to check fluid levels and reconcile inventory. Years of this practice of dropping the sticks would weaken the steel. As a result, exhumed tanks often show accelerated corrosion and holes at the point where the measurements were taken.

The risks of cancer and other disorders increase dramatically when we are exposed to the tremendous variety of chemical compounds and petroleum products released from storage tanks. Exposures to the hazardous materials from tanks can occur for example by vapors migrating into your home, touching soil contaminated by aboveground leaks, and ingestion of pollutants from contaminated water supplies.

Because tanks are associated with just about every type of facility there is, we have effectively "planted" contaminant pods throughout our communities. When the hazardous materials are no longer contained in the tanks, the potential for harmful exposures is significant. As discussed in Chapters 8 and

9, toxic materials can readily migrate through the environment and impact our homes and drinking water supplies.

CONTAMINANT MIGRATION

With underground tanks, the hazardous materials stored inside are already in liquid form and in many circumstances may be buried close to the water table. Leaks from the tanks, therefore, can readily and extensively impact water quality. In cases where petroleum contamination results (especially in groundwater or drinking water wells), it is not always an easy task to identify the responsible tanks. With such a large number of tanks, it can be a difficult process to trace a contamination plume to the source. However, in some instances, such as gasoline leaks, the petroleum can be "fingerprinted" to try to identify an oil company's particular blend or age of gasoline.

Discharges of petroleum and other substances from tank systems can exist in and migrate through the subsurface in four phases, 1) as a free liquid, 2) as dissolved contamination in water, 3) as a vapor, and 4) adsorbed onto soil particles. Because of the variable phases and subsurface irregularities, tank leaks can migrate in highly unpredictable directions. The migration of a discharge depends upon the quantity released, the physical characteristics of the contaminant (such as viscosity and solubility), and the surrounding soil types and moisture conditions.

Estimates of contaminant migration are possible with knowledge of the contaminant type and with an understanding of the geology and hydrogeology of the area. However, the presence of utility lines, variable fill materials, and adjacent foundations can all accelerate the spread or the pooling of a release. These alterations in contaminant migration are because of the more permeable and porous soil found in backfill along utility lines and around the foundations of buildings and homes.

The potential also exists for a release to enter utility piping, such as sewer lines, through breaks in the pipes or through faulty seals. Under fortunately rare circumstances, the pollutants can seep into a home as vapors or even as liquid petroleum and appear in drains, toilets, or sinks.   In addition, in unusual circumstances, the vapors of some contaminants such as gasoline can accumulate in homes to explosive levels.

The horizontal migration of vapors can be quite extensive as the contaminants move from areas of high concentration to areas of low concentration.   Just like liquids, vapors will take the path of least resistance and may migrate faster along utility-line backfill and foundations.   Figure 10.1 illustrates potential migration routes of storage tank discharges.

TANKS AROUND THE HOME

Natural gas or fuel oil usually supplies the heating systems of average single-family homes.   Those heated with fuel oil typically have storage tanks that range in size from 275 to 1,000 gallons.   The vast majority of these tanks are 550 gallons in size and virtually all are constructed from steel.   As these tanks may be either aboveground or underground, homeowners need to consider the benefits and drawbacks of each location.

Residential aboveground tanks may be outside, but more conventionally, they are found in basements or in garages.   Usually, interior aboveground tanks are 275 to 350 gallons in capacity.   The primary advantage to an aboveground tank, whether interior or exterior, is that it can be inspected for signs of trouble.   Disadvantages include possibly offensive odors, the loss of space when the tank is in the house, and when it is outside, weather deterioration or other potentially damaging impacts.

Underground tanks can be situated almost anywhere on a property, although in general they are buried just outside a house relatively close to the heating system area.   The disadvantages of an underground tank due to corrosion are obvious.   Advantages include the reduced interior odor potential and increased availability of space, which permits a larger tank, and therefore, less frequent heating oil deliveries.

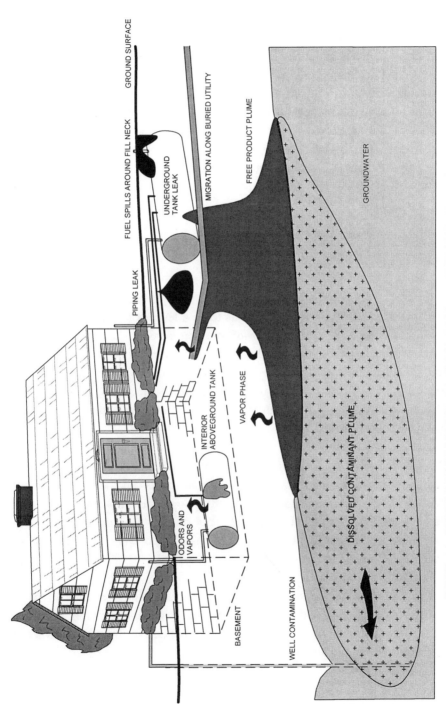

FIGURE 10.1 - POTENTIAL DISCHARGE MIGRATION/EXPOSURE ROUTES FROM STORAGE TANKS

Although aboveground tanks may be more readily inspected for problems, they are far from immune.   I was involved with a project where an aboveground heating oil tank was in a garage. Unfortunately, oil feed lines to the furnace ran across a dirt floor where they were unknowingly damaged. The feed-line piping ended up leaking directly into the soil and underlying bedrock, and ultimately the entire tank contents (and at least one subsequent oil delivery) were discharged into the ground. The oil eventually migrated to and reappeared on the surface of an adjacent lake. What resulted was a costly and invasive cleanup that could have been easily avoided by protecting the exposed feed line.

APPROACH WITH CAUTION

Be prudent if you own or are considering buying a home with an oil tank. During real estate transactions there has to be a level of buyer protection. To prevent the concealment of harmful information, a seller should fully disclose all known conditions relating to the tank.   The information that is disclosed should include a history of releases, operation problems, repairs, and possibly even oil delivery records. A prudent buyer will want the seller to provide indemnification against contamination liability that arises from a failure to disclose relevant information.

During one property assessment, I encountered a homeowner who had purposely buried a number of underground tanks and other hazardous materials on his property in an illegal effort to prevent a bank foreclosure. Although this is an extreme example, it is not rare for new underground tanks to be installed or conversions to natural gas made without removing the former tank - and there it remains, ticking away.

It is important, therefore, to examine a property carefully for indications of out-of-service underground storage tanks. An experienced professional can do the assessment, although common sense and open eyes by a homeowner or prospective buyer can go a long way.

INVESTIGATIONS

Indications that an out-of-service tank may be present on a property can include a number of signs. A fill neck, exterior vent line, and feed/return lines, that are not associated with the current system, may be warning signs. Even a rectangular-shaped area that is depressed a few inches at the surface may indicate an underground storage tank exists and is corroding beneath.

Assuming that a tank is present and acknowledged by a seller, a potential buyer should consider whether or not to keep the tank, replace the tank, or convert to an alternative heating system supply. This decision should be made first to avoid the costs and time associated with investigating for leaks from a tank system that may shortly become obsolete. It is also important because some lenders will not give you a mortgage without an assessment of the tank.

The problem of who pays for an investigation often becomes a point of negotiation with respect to the purchase price. Sale negotiations can become somewhat complicated depending upon the results of the tank investigation. Most purchase contracts should include conditions that allow either party to withdraw from the deal if the findings are not favorable (i.e. it appears that the tank is leaking).

LOW TECH APPROACH TO INVESTIGATIONS

Investigations of the potential for a tank system to be discharging (integrity assessments) can be done in a number of ways - some of which do not cost a dime. Each has advantages and drawbacks. Although it does not provide actual data on leaks in a system, consideration should be given to the age of a tank and the type of surrounding soil and depth to groundwater. Though not always in direct proportion, in general, corrosion is related to age; the older a tank is the more likely problems can develop. Furthermore, variable types of soil around the tank and shallow groundwater can accelerate corrosion significantly, thereby becoming more of a negative factor than simple age.

A measuring stick can be inserted in tanks with a specialized paste that will indicate the presence of water. Due to natural condensation and minor amounts of water in fuel deliveries, it is typical to find up to an inch or so of water in tanks older than twenty years. The water will be found at the bottom of the tank because heating oil is less dense and floats on water. Identification of excessive or increasing amounts of water over time may indicate that the tank system is leaking and that surface water or groundwater is entering the tank or piping.

HIGH TECH APPROACH TO INVESTIGATIONS

Integrity assessments of tanks can be conducted in more detail by volumetric, tracer, and sonic tests that must be performed by professionals. These test methods generally evaluate whether a tank is "tight" based on whether an acceptable or unacceptable rate of leakage is measured.

One type of test requires filling a tank to one hundred percent of its capacity and then measuring changes in oil levels in a standpipe over time. This method compensates for such factors as temperature differentials within the petroleum as well as deflection of the tank ends that could appear to indicate volume changes and possible leaks. Unfortunately, this type of testing can produce uncertain results due to air pockets within the tank and/or possible loose piping and tank fittings.

Other testing systems insert probes into tanks, and by using pressure, vacuum, sonic, and ultrasonic technology, they can detect leaks in the system. Another method of integrity testing involves the addition of "tracer" gases into a tank followed by subsurface sampling for the tracer.

These integrity-check methods have advantages in that they are relatively unobtrusive and can have few accessibility problems. However, as the one method requires a completely full tank, this can be a step in the wrong direction if the tank is already leaking.

The major drawback to integrity testing methods, which attempt to analyze the tank system, is that they cannot determine the actual subsurface conditions outside the tank and piping. By design, they are only reflective of the tank system itself at the time of testing. Therefore, no information is provided with respect to the existence or lack of contamination in the soil around the tank or how long the tank may have been leaking.

Even if system analysis testing indicates a leaking tank, and there is a hole in the tank, it is the location of the hole(s) that actually determines whether a significant discharge will or has occurred. Holes at or near the bottom of the tank may leak almost continuously. Holes in the side or near the top of the tank may leak only when sufficient product level is above the hole to allow the petroleum to escape. Holes in the very top of a tank may not discharge fuel at all, because a tank is rarely (if ever) filled to 100% of its capacity.

System testing also does not furnish any information on residual conditions that may have resulted from a previous tank, or whether there were overfills or spills during product deliveries. Another problem with many test methods is that a "tight" tank is determined as one that has an acceptable rate of leakage, generally less than 0.1 gallons per hour. The question becomes, is any leakage rate acceptable? A tank discharging fuel at an "acceptable rate" for twenty-four hours a day for five, ten, or twenty years or more can add up to an extensive and costly contamination problem.

Assuming that an underground tank is relatively accessible, perhaps the most appropriate integrity assessment method is to conduct actual soil or groundwater sampling. The collection and analysis of samples from around the perimeter of a tank provides direct evidence of the soil conditions, and will also indicate the impact from a previous tank in or near the same location. This type of approach can also be modified to monitor for petroleum vapors in the soil surrounding a tank. If the tank is situated within the water table, samples of the groundwater can be collected for analysis to evaluate if a tank has impacted water quality. Figure 10.2 is a general representation of suspect integrity conditions and some of the tank investigation methods.

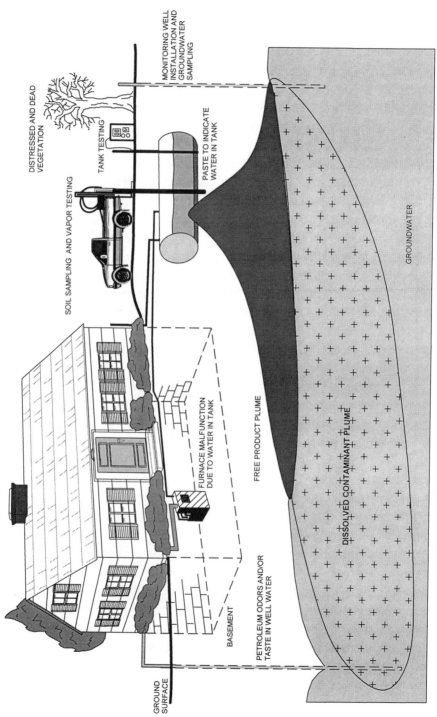

FIGURE 10.2 - INDICATIONS OF TANK LEAKAGE AND COMMON INVESTIGATION METHODS

TANK MANAGEMENT

Ownership of a heating oil tank requires proper operations and maintenance to minimize the potential for a harmful and costly discharge. That includes everything from common sense precautions against damage, to having an awareness of irregularities in system operation, to possibly periodic integrity testing.

PROTECT IT

An electrochemical process that includes the tank, oxygen, moisture, and surrounding soil causes an underground tank and the piping to rust. In most cases, corrosion will occur in multiple places and to varying degrees around the entire tank surface. Something as simple as lumps of clay in sandy backfill around a tank can greatly accelerate corrosion. Consequently, care should be taken to ensure the homogeneity of fill material during tank installation or subsequent excavation work that is performed in the area. The fill material should also be free of angular rocks that under the right conditions can scratch or puncture a tank. Corrosion rates are also affected by such things as imperfections in the steel, dissimilar metals at fittings, and even stray electrical currents in the ground.

In an effort to prevent or at least minimize corrosion, tanks can be covered with a tar-like coating. Additionally, cathodic systems can be added to protect a tank. Cathodic systems typically consist of sacrificial metal (an anode) that is buried and connected to the tank. The purpose is that the anode will corrode rather than the tank.

Although rare on small, residential tanks, other options for ensuring safer operation involve automatic shut-off devices to prevent overfills, and catch basins around fill necks to retain any spills that occur during oil deliveries. Although a tank and the piping may not be leaking, the repeated spillage of just a few gallons around the fill neck can cause a significant problem over the years as the oil accumulates and migrates downward.

Because the pipes (usually copper), which carry fuel to and from a furnace, are at least partially exposed for both aboveground and underground tanks, protecting these pipes is critical. For aboveground tanks in basements, garages, and outside, ensure that the lines are not driven over and that the lines are protected from other forms of damage. In some situations, you may be able to encase the lines within larger diameter protective piping. If feasible, a secondary containment "system" can be constructed around aboveground tanks. This approach may consist of something as simple as a low block wall on an impermeable surface (concrete, asphalt) that will both protect the tank and temporarily contain leaks.

Exterior underground tanks should be buried at least two feet below the ground surface. Tanks that are shallower than this can be susceptible to damage from surface traffic. Driving above a shallow tank with an automobile or heavy lawn tractor can cause the soil to settle and pipes and fittings to flex resulting in damage and leakage. In this same regard, any excavation work in the area of a tank, either by hand or by machine, should be conducted with extreme care.

MONITOR IT

Prudent tank management also involves relatively simple measures to help identify certain conditions that may signify leakage. Excessive water in a tank could signal that a leak is present. Water-indicating paste can be used periodically to check for a meaningful increase in the amount of water. In addition, because the piping intakes for a furnace are usually near the bottom of the tank, irregular furnace operation could be an warning that excess water is finding its way into the tank and is being drawn into the heating system along with oil.

Regular, daily inventory control, such as that conducted at gas stations, is not practical for a residential tank. That requires routine measurements of product levels and estimations of usage rates to determine if oil is "missing" from the tank. However, to a certain degree a fuel-oil supplier for a home conducts a form of inventory control by evaluating the historical oil usage rates by a household in conjunction with weather (temperature) conditions. This information is used to determine when oil deliveries should be necessary. If a tank has run dry or if there is a sharp increase in the amount delivered over past comparable usage periods, your tank may have developed a leak. Nevertheless, this approach would not be able to detect a small, gradual leak that progressed over time (which is most typical) because the leak would be factored into and averaged over normal usage rates.

Most homes use approximately 500 to 1,000 gallons of oil per season. This usage varies of course depending on where you live, the weather patterns, size of the home, efficiency of insulation, and the type of heating system. Use rates that suddenly increase or are much higher than the norm could be cause for concern. Gauges are also available to indicate the quantity of product in a tank. Therefore, if a sudden or relatively rapid product loss were to occur it could be identified rather quickly. A gauge is also effective for monitoring product levels over summer months when the tank is not being used.

Although it would probably be cost prohibitive, it is possible to conduct periodic system integrity testing or soil sampling. The costs of these approaches are between approximately $800 and $2,300 per testing/investigation and reporting. A soil and/or groundwater sampling investigation around a tank is the only method that will most adequately assess the actual impact to the subsurface that may have resulted from a former or current leaking tank.

Several other conditions can develop that should be evaluated to see if your tank system may have a problem. A summary of the primary suspect conditions is as follows:

➤Petroleum odors or taste in well water.
➤Petroleum odors in the home.
➤Dead or distressed vegetation around or above a tank.
➤Inventory discrepancies.
➤Direct evidence of a discharge such as stained soil around the fill neck.
➤Petroleum sheen or oil showing up in basement sumps, or staining and seepage through basement floors and walls.

➤Excessive water in the tank and/or furnace system not operating properly.
➤Need to refill tank in a comparatively short period of time.
➤Failed integrity test.
➤Soil sampling, water sampling, or vapor sampling results that indicate elevated petroleum concentrations.

CLOSE IT OR REMOVE IT

When the investigation of suspect conditions confirms that an underground tank is leaking, at a minimum, stop using the tank immediately. A temporary or replacement heating source will have to be established if removing the tank, and the associated loss of heat, would threaten lives or risk freezing of household piping.

Cessation of tank use should be followed as soon as possible by the removal of all product from the tank. Emptying the tank has the obvious purpose of eliminating the primary source of continuing contamination. The issue of whether the now empty tank should be removed from the ground is influenced by several factors. The actual discharge conditions and local and state regulations will dictate whether any action is necessary, whether a tank can be abandoned in place, or whether it must be removed from the ground. If the tank is readily accessible and has been leaking, the only reasonable approach is to excavate it. Removal (versus abandonment) will allow direct examination of the conditions around and beneath the tank, as well as facilitate the excavation of contaminated soils.

Leaving an obsolete tank in place presents a number of problems. Although the product in the tank may have been removed, inevitably oil sludge and contaminated rusty scale remain in the tank. Unless this material is completely cleaned from the tank, it will serve as a continuing source of soil and possibly groundwater contamination. If a tank is to be abandoned in place (after a thorough cleaning), it should be filled with inert material such as sand or a concrete-like slurry. Filling the tank will eliminate the small potential for subsidence of the ground due to further corrosion and the eventual collapse of the tank.

Closing a tank system because of a leakage problem, replacement, or system conversion, should be done only by professionals. This is not a project for a friend who knows someone with an old backhoe and a hand pump. If the tank is already leaking or is in degraded condition, a bad situation can easily be made worse if proper removal procedures are not followed. In fact, many states require that tanks be handled only by licensed professionals. An additional advantage in using a professional to close a tank is that the procedure and actual conditions can be fully documented in a report. The report will serve as proof to a future buyer that the removal was properly handled and that acceptable residual conditions were reached.

Tank removal procedures are relatively straightforward, though it is critical that they be carefully and properly followed. Piping connected to the tank needs to be drained and flushed and then all product should be pumped from the tank. The tank is then exposed by excavating along the top; at that point the piping is disconnected and capped or removed.

If explosive vapors are in the tank (such as in gasoline), they are eliminated before opening the tank and thoroughly cleaning the interior. The tank is then exhumed and post-excavation samples can be collected to assess the residual soil conditions. If contamination is found, there are a large number of remediation methods available. What is right for your tank and property depends entirely on the site-specific conditions.

ASBESTOS

"A man is rich in proportion to the number of things which he can afford to let alone."

Henry David Thoreau

"Touch not; taste not; handle not"

Colossians. II. 21

WHAT IT IS

Asbestos is a name for a group of naturally-occurring, fibrous minerals that have been incorporated into thousands of building and other products. However, due to increased incidences of lung cancer and other disorders associated with occupational exposures to asbestos (typically at high levels), concerns about the presence of asbestos in homes, schools, and public buildings rose dramatically over the past 15 years.

Unique physical properties such as flexibility, high strength, and heat resistance make asbestos an efficient and durable component in a variety of insulation, fireproofing and other construction materials. Asbestos use in commercial applications and building materials ranged from cigarette filters to fire resistant clothing and textiles, to roofing, siding, insulation and flooring, to electrical system components and automotive brakes. Because few other materials can compare to asbestos in strength and heat resistance, as well as cost to produce, asbestos use was widespread throughout much of the past eighty years.

While manufactured materials may contain asbestos, they do not consist entirely of asbestos. An asbestos containing material (ACM) is classified as any product that includes more than 1% by volume or area of asbestos. Depending on the intended product, asbestos minerals may be combined with cellulose, fabric, plaster, cement, papers, vinyl, plastics and numerous other substances.

WHERE IT IS

In general, the types of asbestos containing materials that may exist in homes can be grouped into three broad categories:

1. *Thermal System Insulation* – ACM used to wrap and insulate piping and plaster-like ACM used to cover boilers and piping elbows.

2. *Surfacing Materials* – spray or trowel applied acoustical insulation, fireproofing and surfacing materials.

3. *Miscellaneous* – wallboard compound, floor and ceiling tiles, mastic (adhesive glues used to lay tiles), and border and trim material.

If available, the original construction plans and specifications for a home may identify the manufacturers and types of materials used in construction and may also indicate whether or not they contained asbestos.

In the late 1970s, the federal government placed a ban on many asbestos-containing building products. Because of the extensive prior use and inclusion of asbestos in so many products, it is common for at least some asbestos containing materials to be present in a large percentage of homes built before the ban.

It is also possible for homes constructed after the ban to include asbestos materials. This possibility is due to builders or other contractors who may have either unscrupulously or inadvertently used older supplies of materials. Figure 11.1 is a general illustration of the many locations in a home that asbestos containing materials may be found.

The most common asbestos containing materials in the home consist of insulating materials, which are layered or corrugated wrapping around pipes and ductwork (typically white to gray in color), and plaster-like coatings on boilers and around piping elbows. Additionally, vinyl asbestos floor tiles, which are 9 inches by 9 inches, and the mastic used to glue the tiles to the subfloor often contain asbestos. Other size tiles may also contain asbestos.

To a lesser degree, ceiling tiles and surfacing substances, like textured paints and patching materials, may be asbestos containing materials. The Consumer Product Safety Commission did not ban the use of asbestos in patching compounds until 1977. Asbestos has also been found in the wall insulation in some homes built before the middle of this century.

Levels of asbestos fibers in the exterior air are generally the result of natural mineral sources as well as motor vehicle brake linings that include asbestos. House shingles and exterior roofing materials may also contain asbestos. However, due to the exterior location of these materials, they present a miniscule health risk because they generally do not impact interior air quality where exposures would be increased.

THE HEALTH RISK

Without question, asbestos has been identified as a known human carcinogen. When disturbed, microscopic asbestos fibers can become airborne where they can possibly be inhaled into the lungs. Exposure to a sufficient quantity of

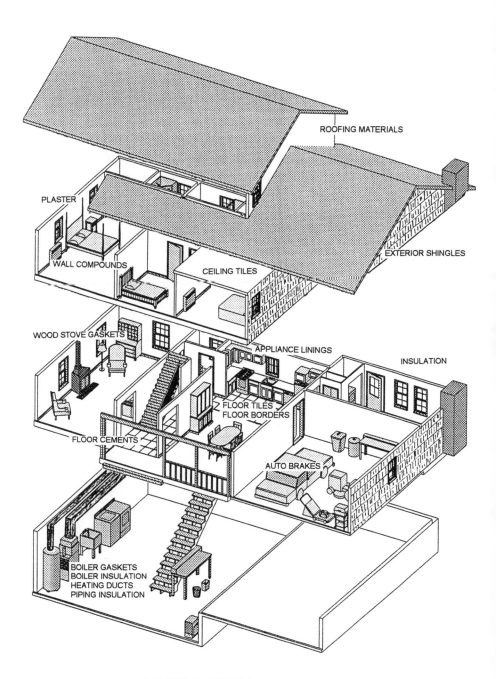

FIGURE 11.1 - COMMON ASBESTOS MATERIAL LOCATIONS

the fibers over a long period has been shown to cause cancer of the lungs and chest lining. However, under normal conditions it is unlikely that these exposure levels would occur in the home.

The EPA has estimated that in the United States, between 3,000 and 12,000 cases of cancer per year (most of them fatal) are linked to asbestos exposure. A 1964 study of U.S. shipyard workers, who were exposed to heavy concentrations of asbestos during World War II, proved that asbestos was responsible for a number of adverse health conditions, many of which took almost twenty years to develop. Asbestos subsequently became the first material ever regulated by the Occupational Safety and Health Administration (OSHA).

ASBESTOSIS AND MESOTHELIOMA

Because asbestos fibers are not broken down by the body, the fibers are tenacious and can cause a variety of serious ailments once inhaled. *Asbestosis* is a condition similar to emphysema; fibrotic scaring of the lung, due to irritation by the asbestos fibers thickens the tissue and significantly reduces lung capacity.

Asbestos fibers can also lodge in the lungs and body cavities and cause a condition known as *mesothelioma*. This is a relatively rare condition in which, as a result of even a limited exposure, inhaled fibers persist and act as a constant irritant over time. Mesothelioma is not a dose-related disease. Ultimately, cancerous cells develop due to the irritation and produce tumors in the lungs and chest linings. Asbestos fibers have also been linked to other lung cancers.

CHILDREN AND ONE MORE REASON TO QUIT

Overall, the potential for exposure of children to asbestos should be of greater concern than the potential for exposure of adults. Most asbestos ailments have latency periods of 10 to 40 years. Consequently, due to the longer life span of children, the potential for the development of disease is a bigger concern than for someone who is much older. These concerns about children, as well as fear of the unknown, hastened much of the school asbestos removal work that began in the 1980s.

As is the case with certain other environmental contaminants, cigarette smoking appears to increase the risks of developing an asbestos-related disease. Fortunately, there appears to be little adverse health effects from the ingestion of asbestos in the form of dust, food or water. Under these circumstances, the body is generally able to expel the fibers.

In view of the inhalation health concerns, the use of asbestos in building and other materials has been greatly curtailed by governmental regulations over the past twenty years. We are at the tail end of a period wherein the use of asbestos in all building materials as well as brake linings is being eliminated.

HOW MUCH IS TOO MUCH?

Despite the known and severe hazards associated with heavy exposures to asbestos in an *occupational* setting, there is little documentation of adverse impacts from typical indoor, residential conditions. This is primarily because the levels of airborne asbestos in the home are tremendously lower than those found in asbestos related workplaces. Home environments have also been shown to be safer because the various asbestos minerals (such as those utilized in home materials versus industry) have significantly differing impacts on the body.

Not all asbestos minerals are created equal. The most widely utilized mineral is known as chrysotile and this type represents as much as 95% of all the asbestos used in asbestos containing materials like piping insulation. Fortunately for us, that while chrysotile has been used so widely, it is not nearly as carcinogenic as other types of asbestos. This differing toxicity is due to the variable sizes and shapes of the asbestos fibers and their relative tendency to lodge within the body.

Typical indoor levels of airborne asbestos fibers are seldom higher than exterior levels (caused by the releases from automotive brakes and other sources). Because asbestos related health conditions are usually proportional to the dose received, low levels have had minimal impact. There has been no report of asbestos-related disease that was due solely to exposure to residential materials.

Because the small interior risk is not quantifiable, the risk of cancer at typical residential levels has had to be extrapolated from much higher industrial exposure levels. The lifetime cancer risk is therefore estimated at less than 1 in 100,000. It is noted that this risk is significantly less than that posed by an unacceptable exposure to radon.

MEASURES TO CONSIDER

Notwithstanding the health hazards that have been demonstrated due to occupational exposures to asbestos, most data indicate typical residential levels should be of limited concern. Regardless of the type of asbestos that may be present, the material can only represent a hazard if it is in some way disturbed to allow the fibers to become airborne and then inhaled.

It is important to note that asbestos is not a radioactive or a biological hazard. We find therefore, that simple close proximity to undisturbed material will not adversely affect one's health. However, asbestos containing materials that have the potential for being disturbed during normal household use or during renovations should be of a higher concern.

If we want to determine if asbestos containing materials are present in our home, the analysis of suspect materials is not an expensive proposition and typical costs per sample are approximately $20. If an entire home is inspected and sampled, the average cost for the complete process and reporting should not exceed $1,500. If sampling of suspect materials is to be performed, a professional should do the work. Without proper training, improper technique can result in the unintended release of airborne fibers and/or result in unrepresentative samples submitted for testing.

Asbestos containing materials such as piping insulation are *friable*, which means they are easily torn or reduced to powder due to physical disturbances. Due to the malleable nature and greater potential for fiber release from friable materials like insulation, they are obviously of greater possible concern than non-friable materials such as floor tile. If suspect material exists in the home or if testing has identified the material as containing asbestos, a survey evaluation of the friability, condition, and the location of the material should be done.

SURVEY

It is a relatively simple task to conduct a home survey to assess the condition of asbestos containing materials, the accessibility, and potential for damage and disturbance. The survey purpose is to evaluate the level of risk that is present or the risk that could develop as related to specific usage circumstances in a home.

Sources of damage and physical disruption of asbestos containing materials include high velocity air flow, water leaks which erode materials, abrasive traffic over floors, a door that swings into a covered pipe, children playing near material, excessive vibration, etc. Asbestos containing material in good condition and in a location where it is improbable that it would be disturbed by outside forces is often better left alone. For example, piping insulation that is in a relatively inaccessible crawl space, in good condition and unlikely to be disturbed, would be of little concern. However, friable asbestos containing materials in close proximity to air vents should be removed; the potential for fiber dispersal throughout a home is greater.

PROTECT

Electric, high efficiency particulate air (HEPA) filters have become increasingly popular and available over the past five years as a means for improving home air quality for allergy sufferers. If concerns exist about uncontrollable asbestos fibers in the air, a HEPA filter can be used to remove the fibers. However, it would be best to eliminate the source of airborne fibers rather than to rely on constant air filtration and the hope that it would intercept fibers before they enter your lungs.

It is also possible to isolate asbestos material that is in good condition but potentially subject to future disruption or disturbance. Small areas can be contained or repaired by wearing an approved respirator and wetting the area first to reduce the potential for generating airborne dust. Piping insulation and other materials can then be covered with protective substances (plaster, metal sheeting, plastic, duct tape) or isolated behind wallboard or paneling.

Asbestos flooring can often be covered over with a new floor. Any future remodeling work with areas that were covered will have to take into consideration the presence of the asbestos. Periodic inspections should be done to ensure no further degradation of the barrier or of the asbestos-containing material occurs. Renovations must consider the potential release of fibers. If insulation, flooring, or other materials are to be affected by work, professional measures should be taken to isolate the work area to prevent fiber dispersal.

Under no circumstances should a suspect floor or the suspect mastic that is left behind after removal of the tiles be sanded. The dust that is created could create a significant airborne hazard.

ABATEMENT

Asbestos containing material that is in poor condition or likely subject to damage should be addressed. For example, material in a basement, laundry, or other room where children play and could disturb the asbestos would be of concern. Any removal (abatement) of significant quantities of asbestos containing material in poor condition is best performed by an experienced and licensed contractor.

Abatements done the wrong way can often release more fibers than if the material were never disturbed in the first place. When properly performed, the abatement contractor should take measures to prevent the release and dispersion of fibers. The contractor should isolate the work area with plastic sheeting and vacuum systems. A small section at a time can be segregated with plastic glove-bags over a length of piping, or an entire room can be segregated with plastic sheeting for larger removal operations. It is also good practice to conduct follow-up air sampling of the house to check for remaining suspended fibers.

DIGGING DEEPER

"Common sense is what tells us the Earth is flat."

Unknown

EXPANDED HOME AND PROPERTY INVESTIGATIONS

Because health risks in a home may originate from known and unknown outside sources as well as from hazardous substances found within a residential property itself, it is often necessary to significantly expand the investigation process. The important question becomes not just what is happening now, but what may have also happened ten, twenty or even eighty years ago

Initially, expanded investigations can consist of research and interviews to provide historical details on the development and use of a property and surrounding area. If the research indicates the possibility for contamination, or if conditions dictate the need for more intensive investigations, a variety of procedures is available to provide a direct assessment of the surface and subsurface environment.

PAPER WORK

Research on the history of a piece of property and the surrounding area comes in many formats. It can range from simple title searches, to document past ownership and use of a piece of property, to aerial photographs that may reveal concerns about the property and surrounding area. Although much of this inquiry can be conducted by anyone with sufficient common sense, the interpretation of the information is often best left to a professional.

SEARCHES

As discussed previously, Community Right-to-Know records provide considerable information on types of hazardous materials that are stored, used and released by industry in an area. This data will also indicate the degree of care that industry is taking to prevent or reduce releases.

Most states compile comprehensive lists of environmental concerns like registered underground tanks and known contaminated sites. These lists may not give extensive details on the circumstances at a particular property, but they do aid in providing data on where hazards may be located and the relative number of contamination problems in one community compared with another. Some states publish annual reports to herald their progress towards identifying and participating in the cleanup of contaminated properties. This type of report provides a comparison basis regarding the aggressiveness with which a particular state addresses contamination problems.

Public databases also provide detailed information on hazardous sites. If concerns exist about a known contaminated site near your home, specific information is available. States maintain case files (that are public property) on the types of contamination, activities, and progress towards cleanup for waste sites. Access to these files usually requires a written request and a subsequent visit to the regulatory offices to review the file. The EPA also maintains Internet listings for Superfund sites that detail the specific conditions and progress being made towards cleanup.

Private companies and consultants also will, for a fee, search state and federal databases. The resulting reports will summarize the number of hazardous waste generators, contaminated sites, registered tanks, etc. within a specific geographic area. Table 12.1 and Figure 12.1 are generalized examples of the information that you can obtain to provide an idea of the proximity of your home to potential contaminant sources. It must be noted, however, that a primary problem with records searches is that the regulatory authority databases are often inaccurate, incomplete, and not up to date. Furthermore, they can only document the sites that they know about. The sites learned about after the fact (like Love Canal) most often create the biggest problems.

TABLE 12.1 - Generalized Summary of Search Results for Environmental Concerns

Type of Site	Number of Sites within Specified Distance from Subject Property			
	Property Itself	0 – ¼ Mile	¼ - ½ Mile	½ - 1 Mile
Underground Tank	1	3	9	11
Superfund Site	0	0	0	1
Leaking Tank	1	1	3	2
Hazardous Waste Generator	0	2	4	6
Solid Waste Landfill	0	0	0	1
Treatment Facility	0	0	1	2
Petroleum Storage	0	0	0	1
Contaminated Site	1	2	1	3
Chemical Storage	0	0	2	0

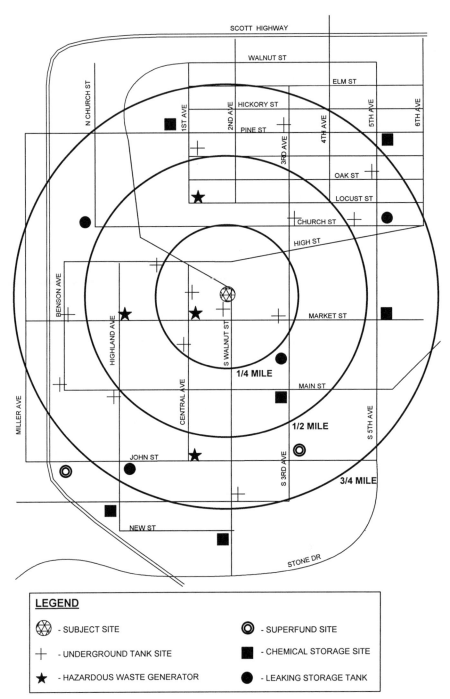

FIGURE 12.1 - SEARCH RESULTS RADII MAP

MAPS AND PICTURES

Historical maps, city directories, and aerial photographs are some of the most valuable resources for documenting the history and the past use of a piece of property. Because the majority of environmental regulations did not exist until the 1980s, it can be a difficult process to assess the potential for historical sources of contamination to have been present on or near a tract of land. Record keeping on environmental matters was minimal compared to today's requirements. Fortunately, mapping and photographic tools can provide an instant glimpse back in time to assess whether historical activities, on or near a property, may have included operations and materials that could have discharged hazardous substances.

The same services that conduct record searches can also provide historical insurance maps. These maps may document the history of a site and the surrounding area for more than 100 years and they often specify the uses of properties, types of construction, and storage of hazardous materials. Historical insurance maps are especially helpful in urban and semi-urban areas, or any area where extensive redevelopment may have occurred. Some city directories also specify the development history of properties dating back as far as the nineteenth century.

In addition to the insurance maps, historical topographic maps by the United States Geological Survey also provide helpful information on previous site usage. These maps can be obtained from the Geological Survey, map services, on CD-ROM, and even at camping stores. Because interpretation of map symbols and plotting to ensure coverage of the correct area can be involved, a consultant should generally do the review and evaluation of the insurance and topographic maps. Figures 12.2 and 12.3 are general representations of insurance maps that illustrate the significant development changes that can occur over time, and the potential concerns that could be associated with the historical site usage.

Virtually every location in the United States has been photographed from the air repeatedly over the years. It is certainly true that a picture is worth a thousand words especially when the picture covers a wide area and gives a

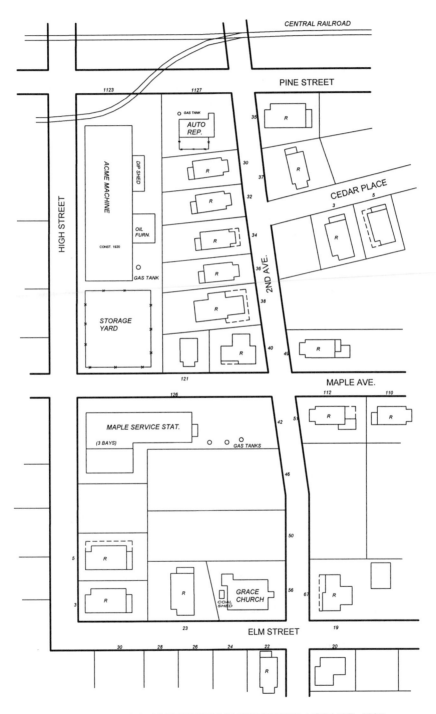

FIGURE 12.2 - HYPOTHETICAL HISTORICAL USE MAP, 1935

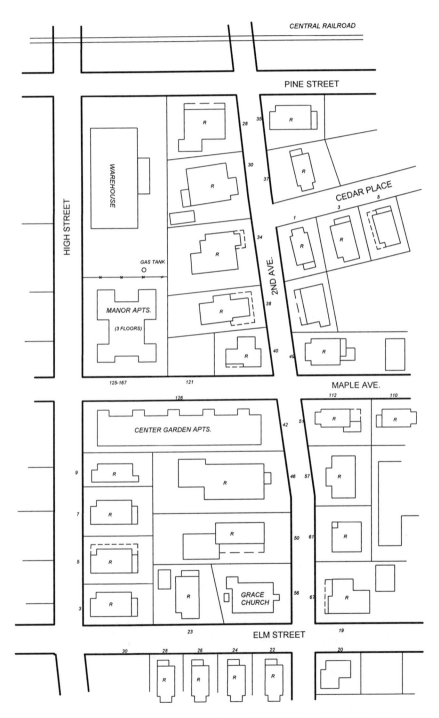

FIGURE 12.3 - HYPOTHETICAL HISTORICAL USE MAP, 1975

bird's eye view. Aerial photographs, taken at the right scale and properly interpreted, provide valuable information on current and historical activities in an area of concern. Because the height of surrounding fences no longer matter from the air, the photographs allow a certain amount of "spying" into the properties of likely polluters.

Copies of aerial photographs can be obtained from state governments, search companies, on the Internet, or directly from aerial photography services. Coverage for most areas is available, although areas that are more rural are photographed less frequently. Some locations may be photographed several times a year while others may be photographed only every five years or so. In general, it is possible to piece together aerial coverage that will give a photographic history dating back as much as fifty years. Figure 12.4 is an aerial photograph that illustrates the intermingling of residential, industrial and commercial usage zones.

LEG WORK

In the event that the paper work portion of an investigation indicates that potentially hazardous conditions may exist, the data can be supplemented with interviews and actual on the ground reconnaissance work. Nothing can surpass concrete, first-hand knowledge in going beyond the research portion of an investigation.

INTERVIEWS

Interviews with neighbors, especially old-timers, can provide a wealth of information with respect to the historical activities in a community. Although it may not be written down or otherwise documented, discussions with the residents of a community can provide good insight as to the operations or waste disposal practices that may have previously existed. Certainly, if the right person at the right time had asked the right questions of a long-time employee of the Hooker Chemical Company, the name Love Canal may never have meant what it means now.

FIGURE 12.4 - AERIAL PHOTOGRAPH

On a local level, fire department, engineering department and health department officials can be interviewed as significant sources of information both on and off the record. State officials can also be questioned about their opinions and information they have on a particular remediation project.

RECONNAISSANCE – TAKE A WALK

Simply by opening your eyes, taking a walk, and using common sense you can investigate and learn more about a piece of property and a community than perhaps you ever wanted to know. When assessing a piece of property, look for the signs of abandoned underground tanks such as rectangular subsidence and unexplained fill necks or vent pipes, etc. As much as is reasonable, extend your observations to neighboring properties. After all, leaks from nearby tanks can cause as much trouble as tanks on the site itself.

During the reconnaissance of a piece of property, check for unusual odors and look for unexplained stains or dying vegetation that may indicate contamination. Unless you are an oil prospector, black goo oozing out of the ground is not a good sign. Pay attention to surface precipitation runoff patterns and the activities of neighbors. Will rain and snow carry someone else's waste oil spills or excessive pesticide onto your property?

A residential neighborhood is not always just a residential neighborhood. Pay attention to activities in the area. I was involved in a case some years ago where almost everything appeared to be a conventional house in a typical suburban neighborhood. However, the owner of the home had installed underground diesel fuel and gasoline tanks to supply his construction business vehicles. The neighbors had never bargained for the fact that they would be living next to what amounted to a service station.

REGIONAL AWARENESS

On a larger scale, driving and walking through a community will provide a considerable amount of information on the environmental health of an area.

When you are filling up at the local gas station, look for the circular metal plates (monitoring well covers) scattered across the pavement and a treatment equipment shed that indicate a groundwater investigation and remediation program.

Attention should also be paid to industrial and commercial facilities. Are 55-gallon drums stored haphazardly on the ground? Are noxious odors coming from the facility? Are two-foot steel pipes (aboveground protective casings for monitoring wells) sticking out of the ground here and there? Are piles of dirt sitting on plastic sheeting? These features suggest at least the potential for contamination or the investigation and cleanup of a problem. The question becomes what is the extent of the impact?

DIRTY WORK

If findings to this point imply that historical contamination may be present on your property, or that an off-site contaminant plume may be impacting it, an even more aggressive investigation could be warranted. The type and degree of this investigation would depend on the potential contaminants that may exist together with the site-specific circumstances.

MAGNETOMETRY

In some cases aerial photographs, site circumstances, or historical mapping may indicate old tanks, hazardous material storage, or even waste dumping. Concerns about the possibility of underground tanks, unknown piping, or other wastes that may be buried in metallic containers can be investigated without ever scratching the surface. Through the use of ferrous object detectors, metals such iron, steel and some alloys can be located due to differences in magnetic fields. These devices are typically more advanced than your average beach treasure finders and can detect items buried as deep as eight feet.

By using a magnetic detector and traversing a property on a set grid pattern, a professional can develop and interpret a map that indicates magnetic anomalies that may warrant further investigation. In cases where a vent line and/or remote fill neck are present, but the whereabouts or existence of the tank are questionable, the locators can connect to and trace the underground piping to verify the presence of a tank.

GROUND PENETRATING RADAR

Somewhat similar in general principle to magnetic surveys, ground-penetrating radar is another non-invasive technique that creates a profile of what may be under the ground. The unit is moved across the ground surface and high-frequency impulses are transmitted into the ground via an antenna. The impulses are reflected by discontinuities in the ground such as drums or a buried tank (fiberglass or steel) and the antenna picks up the reflection. A professional can map a relatively large area, and, when properly interpreted, the profiles can indicate where materials may be buried. If the reflections appear consistent with either tanks or other buried wastes, more invasive investigations are needed.

SOIL AND GROUNDWATER EXPLORATIONS

The only way to finally determine the degree to which a property has been contaminated (either from off-site or on-site sources), is to actually get up close, personal, and probably analytical. If the historical data or other survey findings demonstrate more intensive subsurface explorations are warranted, a consultant should be retained (if you have not already) to evaluate the concerns, the site-specific conditions, and the most appropriate methods for exploration.

Three primary options are available to perform a soil and groundwater exploration and sampling program. A backhoe can excavate test pits - narrow trenches in the ground. This method can cover a considerable area and provides a direct examination of soil and groundwater conditions to typical depths of about ten feet. Samples can be collected easily with this approach and the necessary machinery (a backhoe excavator) is often present during initial site development. Inasmuch as the excavation of test pits is quite invasive, it may not be the best choice for previously developed properties with subsurface utility concerns, finished lawns, etc.

As alternatives to test pit excavations, soil and groundwater conditions can be investigated with a variety of probing and drilling methods. Hand-operated and relatively small systems mounted in the back of a pickup truck are available to advance subsurface sampling devices. Small holes (less than two inches in diameter) are made by drilling or hydraulically pressing and hammering augers and probes into the ground. Soil, groundwater and vapor samples can be retrieved from the holes for inspection, measurements and analytical testing.

Larger drilling rigs, mounted on several ton trucks, can be used to auger into the soil, drive sampling devices, and install groundwater monitoring wells. Simply due to the weight of the larger drill rigs, significant ruts in lawn areas can be common. Although neither of the drilling approaches provides the same open soil profile that you can get with a test pit, they explore to greater depths and the overall disruption is typically much less.

The expense associated with a full-blown site investigation can be considerable. The number of exploratory locations and the number of samples submitted for laboratory analyses vary greatly depending upon the site conditions and the type of contaminant concerns. However, in most cases the costs can be expected to start at $2,500 and can easily exceed $5,000 to $10,000 if the installation and sampling of groundwater monitoring wells is necessary.

TAKING THE PLUNGE

Before conducting any level of home evaluations and before spending what can be a substantial amount of money, the issues of risk assessment and responsibility must be carefully considered and clearly defined. Consider what you want to know, why you want to know it, and what you can do about it. A homeowner needs to arrive at a basic understanding of the range of hazards as well as the mechanisms by which a household can be impacted. Furthermore, consider where the responsibility for an investigation or corrective action belongs. In most of the cases, this is can be more clearly defined with sufficient data.

Whether you are concerned about radon, lead-based paint, underground storage tanks, or household water quality, as you gather data, the risk assessment process should evolve during and at the conclusion of each phase of an investigation. As issues are clarified, you need to re-evaluate each hazard, the potential exposure routes, and what risks you are willing to take. For some people, there is no such thing as being too careful and even minimal reductions in risks are worth almost any effort and expense.

Unfortunately, obtaining the knowledge necessary to make informed decisions is rarely inexpensive or a completely familiar process. However, it is critical to be as fully informed as possible about the environmental risks that may be associated with a home environment. Once informed, you can then make intelligent decisions about accepting the risk or taking the measures that are available to lessen or eliminate a hazard. Your ultimate goal - a safe haven.

APPENDIX - PRELIMINARY HOME SURVEY

RADON

➤ Is there living space below the third floor level?   _____Y _____N

   If yes, as is the case for most homes, the EPA recommends testing.

➤ Do the region of the United States and/or the geology of
the area indicate an increased risk for radon occurrence? _____Y _____N

➤ Does the type of home construction and layout lend
itself to radon accumulation?   _____Y _____N

➤ Has testing for radon been conducted?   _____Y _____N

   If yes: Location_____ Duration_____ Result_____ pCi/L

➤ Who was responsible for the testing and are the results
reliable and representative? _____ _____Y _____N

➤ Is confirmation testing warranted?   _____Y _____N

➤ Is there an active radon reduction system?   _____Y _____N

   If yes, does testing show it is effective?   _____Y _____N

LEAD

➤ What year was the home built? _____

➤ If any, what year were renovations completed? _____

   (Lead-based paint was banned in 1978 and the use of plumbing solder
   with lead was banned in 1988)

➤ Has paint testing been performed?   _____Y _____N

    If yes, did it represent underlying layers?   _____Y _____N

➤ If elevated levels of lead-based paint were detected, consider the exposure risk (especially with respect to children):

    Where is the paint? _____

    What is the condition of the paint? _____Good _____Fair _____Poor

    Potential for accelerated wear/aging of the paint?   _____Y _____N

➤ Could renovations have isolated lead-based paint?   _____Y _____N

➤ Could renovations or an abatement have generated additional lead-based paint dust?   _____Y _____N

➤ Has the water supply been tested for lead?   _____Y _____N

    If elevated water levels were detected, has the source of the lead been identified?   _____Y _____N

    (_____water supply _____supply connections _____household piping)

➤ If elevated water levels are present, is purging effective in reducing lead concentrations?   _____Y _____N

    (First water: _____ ug/l   Purged water: _____ ug/l)

AIR QUALITY

➤ Are sources of carbon monoxide in the home?   _____Y _____N

    If yes, has the home been inspected for potential carbon monoxide accumulation?   _____Y _____N

➤ Are carbon monoxide monitors present?   _____Y _____N

➤ Are volatile organic vapor sources present?   _____Y _____N

➤ Are there indications of mold growth or are conditions present that are conducive to mold growth?   _____Y _____N

➢ Is the home impacted by local sources of air pollution? _____Y _____N

➢ Are there regional air quality concerns?   _____Y _____N

➢ Do weather patterns and/or topographic features
adversely affect regional air quality?   _____Y _____N

CONTAMINATION CONCERNS

➢ Are the state and community responsive to environmental
contamination problems?   _____Y _____N

➢ Are there indications of contaminated site cleanups in
the community?   _____Y _____N

➢ Are there indications of improper or illegal discharges in
the community?   _____Y _____N

➢ Is there reasonable potential for impact to the home due
to transportation accidents or inadvertent discharges?   _____Y _____N

➢ Was imported fill material used to develop the site?   _____Y _____N

  If yes, are there concerns over the fill quality?   _____Y _____N

➢ Is the property subject to contaminants from runoff?   _____Y _____N

DRINKING WATER

➢ Observations:

  Water taste:_____

  Water odor:_____

  Water appearance: _____

  Other indications of potential problems: _____

  _____

➢ What type of system supplies water to the home?

      _____Public: Do concerns exist about the quality
               of the water source?   _____Y _____N

               Has monitoring revealed violations
               of the SDWA?   _____Y _____N

               If yes, were the violations significant? _____Y _____N

      _____Private: Do concerns exist about the quality
               of the water source?   _____Y _____N

               Does the water meet potability
               criteria?   _____Y _____N

               Is the well head secure from possible
               surface contamination?   _____Y _____N

➢ Has water testing identified specific contaminants?   _____Y _____N

➢ If contaminants have been identified, is treatment of the
water supply necessary?   _____Y _____N

➢ If treatment is ongoing, does testing show it to be
effective?   _____Y _____N

➢ Is an alternate water source warranted?   _____Y _____N

STORAGE TANKS

➢ Is the home heating system supplied by oil contained in
a storage tank?   _____Y _____N

     If no, was the heating system previously supplied
     by an oil tank?   _____Y _____N

     If yes, and the tank was underground, is there
     documentation of proper tank closure?   _____Y _____N

     If no, are there indications of an abandoned tank?   _____Y _____N

➤ What is the status of an active tank?

    Location:_____

    Tank size: _____

    Contents (quantity and fuel type):_____

    Indications of potential problems:_____

    _____

➤ Has a tank investigation been performed?   _____Y _____N

    If yes, was positive integrity demonstrated?   _____Y _____N

    Confidence in findings: _____High _____Moderate ____Low

➤ Are there relatively high numbers of storage tanks in
the community?   _____Y _____N

ASBESTOS

➤ Are suspect materials present?   _____Y _____N

    Location/Type: _____

    _____

    Condition: _____

    _____

➤ Could renovations have isolated asbestos containing
materials?   _____Y _____N

➤ Has laboratory testing confirmed the presence of
asbestos containing materials?   _____Y _____N

    If yes, are the materials friable and is there reasonable
    potential for exposure if disturbed?   _____Y _____N

➤ Could an improper renovation or abatement have
released airborne fibers?   _____Y _____N

➢ If concerns exist about airborne fibers, has air monitoring
been performed?   _____Y _____N

EXPANDED SITE INVESTIGATIONS

➢ What is the historical use of the property?

_____

_____

Potential concerns: _____

_____

➢ What are the historical uses of the surrounding properties?

_____

_____

Potential concerns: _____

_____

➢ Is historical mapping warranted?   _____Y _____N

➢ Is aerial photography warranted?   _____Y _____N

➢ Have searches identified a relatively high number of
potential contaminant sources?   _____Y _____N

   If yes, is there reasonable potential for exposure?   _____Y _____N

➢ Community interviews:

_____

_____

_____

_____

Potential concerns: _____

➢ Regulatory agency interviews:

_____

_____

_____

_____

Potential concerns: _____

➢ Area reconnaissance:

_____

_____

_____

_____

Potential concerns: _____

➢ Are there site or vicinity concerns that indicate a
non-invasive subsurface investigation may be warranted? _____Y _____N

➢ Are there site or vicinity concerns that indicate a
sampling of soil or groundwater may be warranted?   _____Y _____N

Note: This preliminary survey is not comprehensive and is intended to be used in
conjunction with the text as a general guide to issues that should be considered
during the assessment of a home and property.

GLOSSARY

Abatement - removal operations for asbestos containing material or lead-based paint.

Aboveground storage tank - typically cylindrical or oval steel vessel used to contain heating oil. In a residential environment usually found outdoors or in a basement.

Absorb - assimilation of matter into the pores or structure of another substance.

Acid Rain - precipitation, including snow, that contains dilute amounts of acids formed from air pollutants such as nitrogen oxides and sulfur dioxides. Combustion of fossil fuels is a primary cause.

Acute toxicity - the ability of a contaminant to cause adverse health impacts due to a single *exposure*.

Adsorb - assimilation of matter onto the surface of another substance. Activated carbon is used to adsorb contaminants.

Analytical laboratory - facility for the testing of soil, water, and air samples to determine physical characteristics and chemical composition. Laboratories should be certified in the type of testing offered.

Anemia - a condition that describes a reduction in the oxygen carrying capacity of the blood (see hemoglobin).

Aquifer - a layer or layers of sand, gravel, or rock that yield economically sufficient quantities of water. A primary source of drinking water.

Asbestos - term for a group of natural mineral fibers that due to physical properties of strength and heat resistance were incorporated into many products. Can present an inhalation health hazard.

Backfill - soil, sand, or rock used to level depressions in the ground surface or around foundations and utilities. Backfill from some sources may contain contaminants.

Bedrock - solid rock formations that are generally covered by overburden (soil, sand, clay, and gravel).

Bio-accumulate - tendency of a contaminant to concentrate in organic matter and to potentially pass along the *food chain*.

Brackish - water with a salt content that renders it non-potable.

Carbon Monoxide - chemical formula: CO. Incomplete combustion byproduct gas capable of causing death by asphyxiation.

Chelation - drug therapy used to remove excessive lead from the body.

Chronic toxicity - the ability of a contaminant to cause adverse health impacts due to repeated *exposures*.

Clay - minerals with a diameter less than 0.002 mm. In a hydrated state, clay layers can be *impermeable* and serve as effective barriers to the passage of water and contaminants.

Cluster - higher than average concentration of disease cases within a geographic area. Often indicative of environmental contamination.

Cross contamination - inadvertent transfer of materials during sampling or laboratory analysis that results in findings not representative of the actual conditions.

Degradation - breakdown of contaminants (usually into less toxic forms) by chemical or biological action.

Dihydrogen monoxide - water.

Dose related - adverse health impacts that are proportional to the quantity and/or concentration of a contaminant *exposure*.

EPA - United States Environmental Protection Agency. Federal agency responsible for the protection and cleanup of the environment.

Exposure routes - avenues by which humans can be impacted with pollutants (inhalation, ingestion, absorption, and contact).

Fallout - settling of particles (commonly radioactive) that were formerly suspended in the atmosphere.

Fill neck - aboveground, capped portion of piping connected to a storage tank. Used to replenish oil in the tank and is often an area of contamination due to spillage.

Food chain - a hierarchy of organisms whereby energy and possibly contaminants are transferred by the consumption of lower organisms. Meat eaters are at the top of the food chain while plants are at the bottom.

Fossil fuels - geologically formed substances such as coal, oil, and natural gas that are recovered and then burned to produce energy. A primary source of air pollution.

Ground penetrating radar - non-invasive geophysical technique that can produce a profile of objects beneath the ground surface.

Groundwater - water within the earth between soil grains and within rock fractures. Primary replenishment is the downward movement of precipitation. Commonly used as a drinking water source.

Groundwater gradient - a measurement of the slope of the *water table*, which due to gravity, serves as the primary mechanism of groundwater movement.

Half-life - time it takes for a substance (usually radioactive) to be reduced to half the original quantity.

Hardness - a relative indication (soft or hard) of dissolved mineral content (primarily calcium and magnesium) in water.

Hazardous waste - spent material (usually industrial) that exhibits especially harmful chemical or physical properties.

Hemoglobin - the oxygen bearing protein in red blood cells. Interfered with by contaminants like *carbon monoxide*.

HEPA - high efficiency particulate air filters that have the capability of removing a minimum of 99.97% of particles larger than 0.3 microns (a micron is one millionth of a meter - a human hair is approximately

100 microns in diameter). Used in lead-based paint and asbestos *abatements*.

Herbicide - chemical substance used to kill vegetation. Overuse results in contaminated surface *runoff* that can enter *surface water* and *groundwater*.

Hydrologic cycle - the continuous transfer of water in solid, liquid, and vapor form between the atmosphere, vegetation, water bodies, and groundwater. An understanding of the cycle illustrates the potential for the incorporation of contaminants.

Igneous rock - rock such as granite and basalt, formed from molten material (magma).

Impermeable - characteristic of soil or rock that prevents passage of fluid due to the absence of interconnected void spaces.

Integrity testing - methods for evaluating the soundness of an underground storage tank system.

Landfill - disposal site for the burial of waste materials. Sanitary landfills are constructed with systems for the collection of *leachate* and other safeguards for the protection of *groundwater*.

Leachate - fluid that contains soluble materials (often contaminants) that were incorporated as the fluid passed through a substance. Precipitation that mixes with refuse buried in a *landfill* produces leachate, which can be a primary source of *groundwater* contamination.

Lead pollution - the persistence of lead in the environment and the *food chain* as it accumulates in organic tissue from sources such as industrial combustion, automobile exhaust, and lead-based paint.

Maximum contaminant levels - MCL. Federal standards for the maximum concentration of specific contaminants allowed in drinking water.

Metamorphic rock - rock like gneiss and marble formed by physical and chemical alteration (usually at depth) due to forces such as high temperature and pressure.

Migration - movement of contaminants by any number of methods such as dispersion, diffusion, in solution, airborne, etc.

Monitoring well - assembly drilled into the earth for the purpose of collecting *groundwater* samples for study purposes.

NIMBY – Not In My Back Yard. Refers to an attitude of opposition to the placement of waste disposal or other treatment facilities within your community. NIABY – Not In Anyone's Backyard. Refers to an attitude of opposition to any waste disposal and treatment facilities regardless of location.

Organic vapor detectors - variety of monitoring devices used to identify and measure concentrations of *volatile organic compounds* in the air.

Outcrop - an occurrence of *bedrock* at the ground surface. In fractured rock, it can represent an avenue for the deep *migration* of contaminants.

pH - measurement of acidity or alkalinity.

PPB - parts per billion, common expression for the concentration of a contaminant in water.

PPM - parts per million, common expression for the concentration of a contaminant in water and soil.

Permeability - the capacity of geologic materials to transmit a fluid (gas or liquid). Clay layers and solid rock may be *impermeable* while gravel and sand have high permeability.

Pesticide - chemical substance used to kill insects, rodents, etc. Overuse results in contaminated surface *runoff* that can enter *surface water* and *groundwater*.

Petroleum (petroleum hydrocarbons) - general term for oil, gasoline, diesel fuel, etc. consisting primarily of carbon and hydrogen. Common contaminant due to widespread use and leakage from storage tanks.

Photochemical smog - caused by the reaction of sunlight with combustion emissions (typically automobile). A major source of air pollution.

Plume - concentrations of contaminants that have the capability of *migration* through the air, soil, or water. Plume shape is dictated by proximity to the contaminant source, contaminant type, geological features, and other factors.

Pore space - voids within soil materials. May be occupied by either water or air. When entirely saturated with water, represents the *water table*.

Potable - water suitable for consumption.

Private water supply - typically represented by a single *production well* for a residence.

Production well - assembly drilled into the earth for the purpose of retrieving *groundwater* for drinking purposes.

Public water supply - municipal or commercial service that furnishes drinking water to multiple customers from either *surface water* or *groundwater* sources.

Remediation standards - target concentrations of contaminants established to determine the acceptable restoration of either soil or water.

Risk Assessment - evaluation of the potential for exposure to and adverse health impacts from environmental hazards. Factors include age, health, lifestyle, *exposure routes*, contaminant concentrations, duration of exposure, etc.

Runoff - fluid flow (usually precipitation) across pavement or the ground surface. Runoff that encounters pollutants on the ground surface or on road surfaces can carry the contaminants into water bodies.

Salinity - used to describe dissolved salts in water. Excessive groundwater withdrawal from coastal wells can result in saltwater intrusions that cause wells to become saline (*brackish*) and non-*potable*.

Sedimentary rock - rock such as sandstone and shale. Usually formed due to the deposition and then compression of solid materials (sand, clay).

Soil boring - exploratory method for sampling the ground in contaminant studies such as *integrity testing* and *plume* delineation.

Solvent - liquid which can dissolve other substances. Often petroleum based and highly toxic. Widespread industrial and commercial use and disposal makes solvents a common groundwater contaminant.

Surface water - collective term for reservoirs, streams, and rivers. Major source of drinking water.

Systemic - contaminants that are dispersed throughout a plant or animal.

Test pit - exploratory method that involves the excavation of a narrow trench to expose the soil profile and for sampling purposes.

Toxicity - the potential chemicals and other substances have for causing adverse impacts.

Transpiration - release of moisture into the atmosphere from vegetation.

Underground storage tank - buried vessel (usually steel in a residential environment) designed to contain heating oil.

Volatile organic compounds - general term for a number of petroleum based and other highly *toxic* chemicals that evaporate readily. Because of widespread use, volatile organic compounds are common air, soil, and groundwater contaminants.

Water hardness - a relative description, soft or hard, of the amount of dissolved minerals such as calcium.

Water indicating paste - substance that changes a distinctive color when in contact with water, but is unaffected by petroleum. Useful for assessing the presence of water within storage tanks.

Water table - changeable level below the ground surface where soil pores or rock fractures are completely saturated with water. Also known as the zone of saturation. The water table fluctuates due to precipitation variations, tidal influences, and water withdrawal.

INDEX

NOTES